MEDITERRANEAN
VEGETARIAN COOKING

MEDITERRANEAN VEGETARIAN COOKING

Innovative vegetarian recipes for the adventurous cook

Edited by Janet Swarbrick

APPLE

A QUINTET BOOK

Published by The Apple Press
6 Blundell Street
London N 7 9BH

ISBN 1-85076-666-5

This book was designed and produced by
Quintet Publishing Limited
6 Blundell Street
London N7 9BH

Creative Director: Richard Dewing
Designer: Isobel Gillan
Project Editor: Diana Steedman

Typeset in Great Britain by
Central Southern Typesetters, Eastbourne
Manufactured in Singapore by
Eray Scan Pte Ltd
Printed in Singapore by
Star Standard Industries (Pte) Ltd

The material in this book previously appeared in:
French Country Cooking by John Varnom, *Fruit Fandango* by
Moya Clarke, *Low Fat Cooking* by Pamela Westland,
Mexican Cooking by Robert Hicks, *Meze Cooking* by
Sarah Maxwell, *Natural Cooking* by Elizabeth Cornish,
Nuevo Cubano Cooking by Sue Mullin, *The Encyclopedia of Pasta*
by Bridget Jones, *Portuguese Cooking* by Hilaire Walden,
Spanish Cooking by Pepita Aris, *Tapas* by Adrian Lissen and
Sara Cleary, and *Vegetarian Pasta Cookbook* by Sarah Maxwell.

Contents

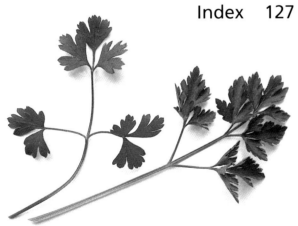

INTRODUCTION

The first pleasures of Mediterranean vegetarian cookery are the wonderful tastes and the natural goodness it brings to your table. The freshness and flavour of natural foods, unrefined and free from additives, offer a range of ingredients that is infinitely rich and subtle. But Mediterranean vegetarian eating doesn't only satisfy the palate, it brings long-term health benefits too.

Our Western diet tends to be soft, sweet and high in animal fat. Over-refined and processed foods contain fewer vitamins and minerals, and chemical additives can cause unpleasant side effects. The foods closest to nature – fresh fruit and vegetables, unrefined grains, nuts and beans – are high in vitamins and minerals, high in fibre, and low in fat. They provide cheaper protein and satisfy at moderate calorie levels.

It is not only the total of fat consumed but the type of fatty acids a given food contains that has a deleterious effect on health.

All fats and oils are made up of a mixture of three types of fatty acids in varying proportions. And indeed all foodstuffs, even fruit, vegetables and grains – those most unfatty-seeming of ingredients – contain a small proportion of all three types of fatty acids.

Saturated fats, principally derived from meat and meat products (such as lard), and from dairy products (including milk, cream, butter and cheese) are known to raise blood cholesterol levels.

Polyunsaturated fats are largely derived from vegetable sources, such as peas and beans (both fresh and dried), nuts and seeds, sunflower, safflower and corn oils, and also from fish and fish oils, and they can actually contribute to the lowering of the cholesterol level.

Monounsaturated fats found in avocados and in olive oil, which is used extensively in Mediterranean cookery, have not as yet been found to play a significant part either way in the deleterious- or beneficial-to-health debate.

So a wholefood diet not only tastes delicious – it also offers protection against common Western diseases, such as heart attacks, obesity, tooth decay and ailments of the lower digestive system.

When the interest in healthy eating first gained momentum, we were encouraged to chew our way through vast amounts of raw food because it did us good. But vegetarian cooking is delicious and this is a frequent surprise to dedicated meat-eaters. For a modest outlay you can stock your cupboard with beans and grains, honey and molasses, fruit and vegetables, and fill your refrigerator with fruit, fruit juices, yogurt and cheese.

Salads exemplify the Mediterranean way of life, and an exciting array of vegetarian dishes are served at every café in the region.

Vegetarian cheeses, made with vegetable rennet, are becoming increasingly available in many different flavours and textures. If the particular cheeses recommended in the recipes are not available in a vegetarian form, you can simply use another type.

Rice and pasta cooked with vegetable oils, cheese and vegetables result in excellent healthy foods abounding in a dietician's delight of minerals, vitamins and other nutritive goodies. Pasta embellished with fresh vegetables and other nutritious food is a delicious preventative measure to take against heart disease and cancer.

A point to note is to beware of certain coloured pastas that are not vegetarian. For example, black pasta will probably be dyed with squid ink.

Mediterranean Vegetarian Cooking provides you with exciting, new and interesting recipes, some of which are quick and simple to prepare, while others require a little extra time and effort for those special-occasion meals. Whether you're cooking for a group of vegetarian guests or the odd one out in the family, these recipes will give you plenty of mouth-watering ideas.

In Mediterranean regions, vegetarian dishes are served at every café, in every house, and on many a street corner. They can be anything from a small nibble of toasted pumpkin seeds to a whole array of tempting salads, dried-bean dishes, dips, tiny kebobs, vegetables – stuffed and unstuffed – and much more, creating a wealth of colours, tastes and textures, all chosen to complement and enhance one another.

This book provides an extensive range of dishes to serve at the table. Some of the recipes are traditional, others classic, and still more are adaptations – with the use of a little poetic licence – in which substitutions for ingredients or changes in methods of cooking have occasionally been made so that the recipes are more accessible.

Whenever you feel like adding a taste of the Mediterranean to the occasion, any one of the dishes can be added to a menu, prepared for a light lunch, or served as an appetizer or a dessert. You may want to increase the quantities of ingredients if, say, one dish is to be served as a main course on its own (remember to allow for extra

En route to the market place. An unparalleled selection of fresh fruits, vegetables, oils and beans are available to the vegetarian cook.

cooking time too). That's the wonderful thing about Mediterranean cooking – you can always add a little extra of one thing or another if you have an unexpected guest arrive, or you simply want the dish to stretch a little bit further.

Vegetarian cooking exemplifies the Mediterranean way of life – it's relaxed in every aspect. There is no particular way to serve most dishes; you simply pick and choose the ones you like best, lay them and invite one and all to help themselves. Most of the dishes can be prepared in advance, others can be left to simmer or be reheated just before serving – so whatever the occasion, with Mediterranean vegetarian food you'll be sure to have plenty of time to enjoy the preparation.

APPETIZERS, SOUPS AND SALADS

Pumpkin Soup with Courgettes

Gazpacho

Creamy Chestnut Soup

Pasta and Pea Soup

Clear Mushroom Soup

Pasta Bean Soup

Classic Greek Vegetable Soup

Tomato Pasta Timbales with Basil Sauce

Aubergine and Mushroom Pâté

Starfruit and Rocket Salad

Greek Potato Salad

Classic Greek Salad

Riviera Salad with Pineapple and Ginger Dressing

Tortellini, Peppers and Pine Nut Salad

Spinach and Fig Salad

Baked Salad of Red Peppers and Tomato

Layered Tomato and Pasta Salad

Shredded Vegetable and Linguine Salad

Pasta Salad with Fresh Dates

Yogurt with Passion Fruit and Cucumber

Herbed Mushroom Pasta Salad

Stuffed Pasta Shells

PUMPKIN SOUP WITH COURGETTES

SERVES 4

Replacing animal fats with sunflower oil significantly reduces cholesterol content of any dish. When only half of the vegetables are puréed, as in this recipe, the soup has a more interesting texture and a more appetizing appearance.

1 tbsp sunflower oil

1 medium onion, chopped

350 g/12 oz pumpkin or squash, peeled, seeded, and diced

225 g/8 oz carrots, diced

2 potatoes, peeled or scrubbed and diced

700 ml vegetable stock

2 courgettes, thinly sliced

freshly ground black pepper

Garnish

2 tbsp chopped parsley

≈ Place the oil and onion in a saucepan, and cook over medium heat for 2–3 minutes to soften the onion. Add the pumpkin or squash, carrots, potatoes, and stock. Bring to the boil, cover, and simmer for 15 minutes, or until the vegetables are nearly tender. Add the courgettes and cook for another 5 minutes.

≈ Purée half of the soup in a blender or food processor, stir the purée into the remaining soup, and season with salt and pepper to taste. Reheat the soup if necessary, and serve in individual bowls. Make sure that some of the courgette slices float on top to decorate the soup. Sprinkle with parsley and serve piping hot.

NUTRITION FACTS	
Amount per Serving	
Calories 135	Calories from Fat 27
	% Daily Value
Total Fat 3g	5%
Saturated Fat 0.5g	2.5%
Polyunsaturated Fat 2g	0%
Monounsaturated Fat 0.5g	0%
Cholesterol 0mg	0%
Sodium 22mg	1%
Total Carbohydrate 23g	8%
Dietary Fibre 5g	20%
Sugars 7g	0%
Protein 3g	0%

Percent daily values are based on a 2000 calorie diet

GAZPACHO

SERVES 4

A favourite soup of Southern Europe, gazpacho can have more bread added to make it more substantial.

450 g/1 lb large ripe tomatoes

1 large onion

2 cloves garlic

1 green pepper

1 red pepper

½ cucumber

2 slices wholewheat bread,
   crusts removed

3 tbsp olive oil

3 tbsp wine vinegar

285 ml/½ pt tomato juice

285 ml/½ pt water

salt and freshly ground black pepper

≈ Skin tomatoes, discard seeds and juice and chop the flesh. Peel and finely chop the onion and garlic. Remove pith and seeds from peppers; dice. Peel and dice the cucumber. Dice the bread.

≈ Put vegetables and bread in a large bowl, pour over the remaining ingredients, stir and season. Chill well – overnight is best for a good tasty soup.

≈ You can partly blend the soup if you wish, or blend all of it, in which case offer small bowls of chopped onions, tomatoes, peppers, cucumber and croutons as a garnish.

NUTRITION FACTS	
Amount per Serving	
Calories 188	Calories from Fat 80
	% Daily Value
Total Fat 9g	14%
Saturated Fat 1g	5%
Polyunsaturated Fat 1g	0%
Monounsaturated Fat 6g	0%
Cholesterol 0mg	0%
Sodium 290mg	12%
Total Carbohydrate 21g	7%
Dietary Fibre 7g	28%
Sugars 13g	0%
Protein 5g	0%

Percent daily values are based on a 2000 calorie diet

CREAMY CHESTNUT SOUP

SERVES 4

Chestnuts often replace beans in Mediterranean cooking and they are used in the same way as potatoes are elsewhere in Europe. Here they make a delicious, creamy winter soup, delicately flavoured with a little cinnamon.

450 mg/1 lb chestnuts unshelled or
    350 mg/12 oz shelled

salt and freshly ground black pepper

1 thick slice of bread

4 tbsp olive oil

2 tbsp red-wine vinegar

625 ml/1¼ pt light stock

⅛ tsp cinnamon

NUTRITION FACTS	
Amount per Serving	
Calories 275	Calories from Fat 117
	% Daily Value
Total Fat 13g	20%
Saturated Fat 2g	10%
Polyunsaturated Fat 2g	0%
Monounsaturated Fat 9g	0%
Cholesterol 0mg	0%
Sodium 67mg	2.8%
Total Carbohydrate 37g	12%
Dietary Fibre 4g	16%
Sugars 6g	0%
Protein 3g	0%

Percent daily values are based on a 2000 calorie diet

≈ If unshelled, slash the chestnut shells in an x-shape across the fat part of the nut, drop into a pan and cover with cold water with a little salt. Bring to the boil and cook for 20 minutes. Let them cool (but leave under water).

≈ Peel the chestnuts, removing brown skin too.

≈ Fry the bread in the oil then put it in a blender or food processor and purée with the vinegar. Reserve a handful of coarse nuts (chopped) to add texture to the soup and add the rest to the blender, a little at a time, with some of the stock. Purée to a cream. Return the creamed soup to the pan, taste and season with salt and pepper. Flavour discreetly with the cinnamon. Add the chopped nuts, heat through and serve.

PASTA AND PEA SOUP

SERVES 4

A simplified version of Italian minestrone, this recipe uses wholewheat pasta spirals which have a higher fibre content than regular pasta. You could substitute any other pasta shapes you have.

1 medium onion, chopped

1 clove garlic, crushed

2 celery sticks, finely chopped

2 medium carrots, thinly sliced

1 bouquet garni

2 bay leaves

170 ml/6 fl oz tomato juice

600 ml/1 pt water

140 g/5 oz wholewheat pasta spirals

175 g/6 oz frozen peas

⅓ tsp mixed herbs

1 tsp paprika

salt

Garnish

few sprigs coriander or parsley
(optional)

≈ Place the onion, garlic, celery, carrots, bouquet garni, bay leaves, tomato juice and half the water in a large saucepan. Bring to the boil, lower the heat, cover, and simmer for 5–6 minutes.

≈ Add the remaining water, pasta, peas, herbs and paprika. Bring to the boil and simmer for 8–10 minutes until the pasta is tender. Season to taste.

≈ Serve piping hot in individual bowls, garnished with fresh herbs if you wish.

NUTRITION FACTS	
Amount per Serving	
Calories 158	Calories from Fat 18
	% Daily Value
Total Fat 2g	3%
Saturated Fat 0.3g	1.5%
Polyunsaturated Fat 1g	0%
Monounsaturated Fat 0.2g	0%
Cholesterol 0mg	0%
Sodium 47mg	2%
Total Carbohydrate 28g	9%
Dietary Fibre 13g	52%
Sugars 8g	0%
Protein 10g	0%

Percent daily values are based on a 2000 calorie diet

CLEAR MUSHROOM SOUP

SERVES 4

This is a formal soup for special occasions. It has a strong mushroom flavour with the delicate addition of vegetables and pasta to create the contrasting textures.

25 g/1 oz dried mushrooms

600 ml/1 pt warm water

1 leek

1 carrot

80 g/3 oz conchigliette piccole (tiny pasta shells), cooked

salt and freshly ground black pepper

flat parsley leaves to garnish

≈ Place the mushrooms in the warm water, and leave to soak for about 30 minutes. Drain the mushrooms, reserving the liquid in a saucepan.
≈ Slice the mushrooms, and shred the leek and carrot. Add the vegetables to the mushroom stock and cook over a medium heat for about 10 minutes, until the vegetables are tender.

≈ Add the cooked pasta shells, and season with salt and freshly ground black pepper. Cook for a further minute. Serve garnished with parsley leaves.

NUTRITION FACTS	
Amount per Serving	
Calories 37	Calories from Fat 6
	% Daily Value
Total Fat 0.7g	3%
Saturated Fat 0.1g	0.5%
Polyunsaturated Fat 0.4g	0%
Monounsaturated Fat 0g	0%
Cholesterol 0mg	0%
Sodium 10mg	0.4%
Total Carbohydrate 5g	1.6%
Dietary Fibre 3g	12%
Sugars 3g	0%
Protein 3g	0%

Percent daily values are based on a 2000 calorie diet

PASTA BEAN SOUP

SERVES 4

*A nutritious meal in itself – low-fat and full of protein.
Serve with warm, crusty garlic bread.*

2 tbsp olive oil

3 cloves garlic, crushed

4 tbsp chopped fresh parsley

175 g/6 oz dried wholewheat gnocchi piccoli (shells) pasta

3 l/6 pt vegetable stock

3 tbsp tomato paste

350 g/14 oz can mixed beans, such as borlotti, cannellini, etc

salt and freshly ground black pepper

freshly grated Parmesan cheese

≈ Heat the olive oil in a large saucepan, and sauté the garlic with the chopped parsley for about 2 minutes. Add the pasta and cook for 1–2 minutes, stirring constantly.
≈ Pour in the vegetable stock, and add the tomato paste. Bring to a boil, reduce the heat, then simmer for about 10 minutes, stirring occasionally, until the pasta is tender.

≈ Add the beans, and season with salt and freshly ground black pepper. Continue to cook for a further 5 minutes, then serve with a little freshly grated Parmesan cheese.

NUTRITION FACTS	
Amount per Serving	
Calories 338	Calories from Fat 90
	% Daily Value
Total Fat 10g	15%
Saturated Fat 1g	5%
Polyunsaturated Fat 1g	0%
Monounsaturated Fat 4g	0%
Cholesterol 3mg	1%
Sodium 432mg	18%
Total Carbohydrate 52g	17%
Dietary Fibre 11g	44%
Sugars 6g	0%
Protein 14g	0%

Percent daily values are based on a 2000 calorie diet

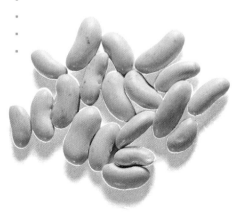

CLASSIC GREEK VEGETABLE SOUP

SERVES 6

Serve this classic Greek soup with freshly baked olive bread.

110 ml/4 fl oz olive oil

2 garlic cloves, crushed

2 onions, finely chopped

½ cabbage, finely shredded

3 carrots, chopped

3 celery sticks, chopped

2 large potatoes, peeled and diced

3 l/5 pt vegetable stock or water

4 tomatoes, peeled, seeded, and
   chopped

salt and freshly ground black pepper,
   to taste

4 tbsp chopped fresh parsley

50 g/2 oz feta cheese, grated

≈ Heat the olive oil in a large saucepan and add the garlic and onion. Cook for 5 minutes, until the onion is softened but not coloured. Add the cabbage and continue to cook for 3–4 minutes.

≈ Add the carrots and celery to the saucepan, stir and cook for a further 5 minutes. Add the potatoes, stir and cook gently for another 5 minutes, until the vegetables are softened.

≈ Pour in the vegetable stock or water and stir well. Increase the heat to bring the soup to the boil. Cover and simmer for 12–15 minutes. Add the tomato and season to taste with salt and freshly ground black pepper. Re-cover and gently simmer the soup for about 1 hour. Stir in the parsley just before the end of the cooking time. Serve sprinkled with grated cheese.

NUTRITION FACTS	
Amount per Serving	
Calories 280	Calories from Fat 190
	% Daily Value
Total Fat 21g	48%
Saturated Fat 4g	20%
Polyunsaturated Fat 2g	0%
Monounsaturated Fat 14g	0%
Cholesterol 6mg	2%
Sodium 151mg	6%
Total Carbohydrate 21g	7%
Dietary Fibre 6g	24%
Sugars 8g	0%
Protein 5g	0%

Percent daily values are based on a 2000 calorie diet

TOMATO PASTA TIMBALES WITH BASIL SAUCE

SERVES 4

An attractive first course, these timbales are sure to impress your guests. Make them up to one hour in advance and place them in the oven to bake.

350 g/12 oz dried, multicoloured
  spaghettini
olive oil
4 small tomato slices
2 tbsp tomato pesto
2 eggs, beaten
60 ml/2 fl oz milk
salt and freshly ground black pepper

Sauce
225 g/8 oz carton passata
1 tbsp soy sauce
4 tbsp chopped, fresh basil
salt and freshly ground black pepper

Garnish
fresh flat parsley sprigs
cherry tomatoes

≈ Bring a large saucepan of water to the boil, and add the spaghettini with a dash of olive oil. Cook for about 10 minutes, stirring occasionally, until tender. Drain.

≈ Preheat the oven to 170°C/325°F/ Gas Mark 3. Grease four 175 ml/6 fl oz ovenproof moulds with olive oil, and place a circle of waxed paper in the bottom of each. Place a slice of tomato in the base of each mould, then pack in the spaghettini, leaving space at the top.

≈ In a small bowl, combine the tomato pesto, eggs, milk, salt and black pepper. Beat well then pour into each spaghettini mould, covering the pasta.

≈ Arrange the moulds in a roasting pan with enough boiling water to come halfway up the sides. Bake for about 40 minutes, until set and firm to the touch.

≈ Meanwhile, to make the sauce, place all the ingredients in a saucepan and heat to simmering point. Simmer for 10 minutes, until thickened slightly.

≈ Run a sharp knife around the edges of each timbale, then invert each onto individual plates. Pour a little sauce around each timbale, and garnish.

NUTRITION FACTS	
Amount per Serving	
Calories 418	Calories from Fat 90
	% Daily Value
Total Fat 10g	15%
Saturated Fat 2g	10%
Polyunsaturated Fat 2g	0%
Monounsaturated Fat 4g	0%
Cholesterol 123mg	38%
Sodium 115mg	5%
Total Carbohydrate 69g	23%
Dietary Fibre 3g	12%
Sugars 7g	0%
Protein 17g	0%

Percent daily values are based on a 2000 calorie diet

AUBERGINE AND MUSHROOM PÂTÉ

SERVES 4

Vegetable pâté is a good, healthful alternative to meat-based pâtés, and makes a filling opening course. The vegetables are high in fibre and free of cholesterol.

1 large aubergine

1 tbsp olive oil

2 cloves garlic, crushed

125 g/4 oz button mushrooms,
    trimmed and chopped

2 tbsp chopped coriander

¼ tsp grated nutmeg

pepper

2 tsp lemon juice

2 tomatoes, skinned, seeded and
    chopped

4 tbsp wholewheat bread crumbs

Garnish

lettuce leaves

cucumber slices

tomato wedges

wholewheat toast

NUTRITION FACTS	
Amount per Serving	
Calories 61	Calories from Fat 27
	% Daily Value
Total Fat 3g	5%
Saturated Fat 0.5g	2.5%
Polyunsaturated Fat 0.5g	0%
Monounsaturated Fat 2g	0%
Cholesterol 0mg	0%
Sodium 55mg	2%
Total Carbohydrate 6g	2%
Dietary Fibre 3g	12%
Sugars 2g	0%
Protein 2g	0%

Percent daily values are based on a 2000 calorie diet

≈ Set the grill to medium. Pierce the aubergine with a fork and place under the grill. Cook until the skin begins to split and the flesh has softened. Turn three or four times to cook it evenly on all sides.

≈ Place the olive oil, garlic and mushrooms in a saucepan, and cook for 2 minutes. Drain off any excess liquid. Add the coriander, nutmeg, pepper and lemon juice, and mix well.

≈ Scoop the flesh from the aubergine, place it in a sieve and press lightly with a spoon to remove the excess moisture. Place the aubergine, mushroom mixture, and tomatoes in a blender and process until smooth. Mix in the breadcrumbs.

≈ Place the mixture in a bowl, cover, and chill for 1–2 hours.

≈ Serve the pâté garnished with lettuce, cucumber and tomato, and with fingers of wholewheat toast.

STARFRUIT AND ROCKET SALAD WITH RASPBERRY DRESSING

SERVES 4

This makes a very good side salad or appetizer. Rocket has a strong, very distinctive flavour which is excellent when balanced with sweet salad greens such as iceberg or cos lettuce, but do not be tempted to add too much rocket or cut it too coarsely as it will overpower the other delicate ingredients, especially the starfruit. If rocket is not available a bunch or two of watercress may be used instead.

½ iceberg lettuce, shredded

12 medium rocket leaves, finely
  shredded

3 spring onions, chopped

2 starfruit, sliced and quartered

Dressing

3 tbsp raspberry vinegar

1 tsp caster sugar

salt and freshly ground black pepper

8 tbsp olive oil

≈ Toss the lettuce, rocket and spring onions together in a salad bowl. Next make the dressing: place the vinegar in a basin and whisk in the sugar with plenty of seasoning. Continue whisking until the sugar and salt have dissolved. Slowly add the olive oil, whisking all the time to combine the ingredients well.

≈ Add the starfruit to the salad. Pour the dressing over and mix lightly. Serve at once. Do not leave the starfruit to stand for any length of time once it is cut since it dries on the surface and tends to discolour slightly around the edges.

NUTRITION FACTS	
Amount per Serving	
Calories 237	Calories from Fat 200
	% Daily Value
Total Fat 22g	34%
Saturated Fat 3g	15%
Polyunsaturated Fat 2g	0%
Monounsaturated Fat 16g	0%
Cholesterol 0mg	0%
Sodium 4mg	0.2%
Total Carbohydrate 8g	3%
Dietary Fibre 1.5g	6%
Sugars 8g	0%
Protein 1g	0%

Percent daily values are based on a 2000 calorie diet

GREEK POTATO SALAD

SERVES 4

Make this salad up to two days before eating it, keep it covered in the refrigerator, and forget about it until required. The flavours will be much stronger when it comes to serving.

900 g/2 lb small new potatoes, scrubbed

1 medium red onion, finely sliced into rings

50 g/2 oz kalamata olives

4 tbsp olive oil

2 tbsp red-wine vinegar

salt and freshly ground black pepper, to taste

1 tsp dried thyme

NUTRITION FACTS	
Amount per Serving	
Calories 278	Calories from Fat 117
	% Daily Value
Total Fat 13g	20%
Saturated Fat 2g	10%
Polyunsaturated Fat 1g	0%
Monounsaturated Fat 9g	0%
Cholesterol 0mg	0%
Sodium 307mg	13%
Total Carbohydrate 38g	13%
Dietary Fibre 4g	16%
Sugars 4g	0%
Protein 4g	0%

Percent daily values are based on a 2000 calorie diet

≈ Place the potatoes in a large saucepan and cover with boiling water. Bring back to the boil and cook for 20–25 minutes, or until the potatoes are tender. Drain and allow to cool slightly.

≈ Cut the potatoes into ½ cm/¼ in slices and arrange in a circular pattern on a serving plate, alternating the potato slices with the onion rings. Scatter the olives over the mixture.

≈ Combine the oil, vinegar, seasoning and thyme in a screw-top jar and shake well to mix. Pour the dressing over the salad. Cover and chill before serving.

CLASSIC GREEK SALAD

SERVES 4

The secret of this internationally famous salad is not in its method, but in its ingredients. You need the freshest of everything to create the feeling of lazy days in the Mediterranean sunshine.

2 large ripe tomatoes

½ cucumber, diced

1 green pepper, seeded and sliced
    into rings

50 g/2 oz kalamata olives

1 large red onion, finely sliced

175 g/6 oz feta cheese, cut into small
    cubes

finely grated zest and juice of
    ½ lemon

4 tbsp olive oil

1 tsp dried oregano

coarsely ground salt, to taste

≈ Cut the tomatoes into thin wedges and place in a medium-sized bowl. Add the cucumber, pepper and olives.

≈ Toss the salad together with half of the red onion slices and half of the cubed feta. Scatter the remaining onions and feta over the top of the salad.

≈ Sprinkle the lemon zest and juice over the mixture, drench with the olive oil, and season with the oregano and salt. Gently toss the salad once just before serving.

NUTRITION FACTS	
Amount per Serving	
Calories 258	Calories from Fat 200

	% Daily Value
Total Fat 22g	34%
Saturated Fat 8g	40%
Polyunsaturated Fat 2g	0%
Monounsaturated Fat 11g	0%
Cholesterol 31mg	10%
Sodium 920mg	38%
Total Carbohydrate 7g	2%
Dietary Fibre 3g	12%
Sugars 6g	0%
Protein 9g	0%

Percent daily values are based on a 2000 calorie diet

RIVIERA SALAD WITH PINEAPPLE AND GINGER DRESSING

Serves 4

An ideal meal-in-moments to enjoy in summertime.

225 g/8 oz green beans, trimmed
salt
4 pineapple rings canned in natural
    juice
4 spring onions, trimmed and sliced
175 g/6 oz low-fat hard cheese,
    diced
12 black olives
½ small lettuce

Dressing

2 tbsp pineapple juice from can
2 tbsp orange juice
large pinch ground ginger
2 tbsp natural low-fat yogurt
salt and pepper

NUTRITION FACTS	
Amount per Serving	
Calories 169	Calories from Fat 72
	% Daily Value
Total Fat 8g	12%
Saturated Fat 4g	20%
Polyunsaturated Fat 0.5g	0%
Monounsaturated Fat 2g	0%
Cholesterol 19mg	6%
Sodium 500mg	21%
Total Carbohydrate 10g	3%
Dietary Fibre 3g	12%
Sugars 9g	0%
Protein 16g	0%

Percent daily values are based on a 2000 calorie diet

≈ Cook the beans in boiling, salted water for 6–8 minutes, until they are just tender. Drain them in a colander, run cold water over them to prevent further cooking, and drain again.
≈ Drain the pineapple, reserving the juice, and cut it into pieces. Mix together the beans, pineapple, spring onions, cheese and olives.

≈ Mix together the dressing ingredients, pour the dressing over the salad, and toss well. Line a serving bowl with the lettuce leaves, and just before serving spoon in the salad. Serve chilled, with hot crusty bread.

TORTELLINI, PEPPERS AND PINE NUT SALAD

SERVES 4

Sweet peppers can be used instead of chilli peppers, if you prefer. For best results, allow the salad to chill for at least an hour before serving.

350 g/12 oz fresh tortellini (stuffed pasta)

dash of olive oil

1 onion, very finely sliced

1 green pepper, seeded and very finely diced

75 g/3 oz toasted pine nuts

1 red chilli pepper, seeded and sliced, or red pepper (optional)

½ cucumber, very thinly sliced

1 orange, peeled and very thinly sliced

Dressing

4 tbsp olive oil

2 tbsp soy sauce

2 tbsp vinegar

salt and freshly ground black pepper

≈ Bring a large saucepan of water to a boil, and add the tortellini with a dash of olive oil. Cook for about 4 minutes, stirring occasionally, until tender. Drain and rinse under cold running water. Drain again and set aside.

≈ Place the tortellini in a large mixing bowl and add the remaining salad ingredients. Toss together lightly.

≈ To make the salad dressing, place the ingredients in a screw-top jar and shake well to combine. Pour the dressing over the salad, toss and serve.

NUTRITION FACTS	
Amount per Serving	
Calories 378	Calories from Fat 225
	% Daily Value
Total Fat 25g	38%
Saturated Fat 5g	25%
Polyunsaturated Fat 6.5g	0%
Monounsaturated Fat 12g	0%
Cholesterol 0mg	0%
Sodium 7mg	0.3%
Total Carbohydrate 29g	10%
Dietary Fibre 3g	12%
Sugars 7g	0%
Protein 10g	0%

Percent daily values are based on a 2000 calorie diet

SPINACH AND FIG SALAD

SERVES 4

450 g/1 lb fresh spinach, washed

25 g/1 oz pine nuts

3 fresh figs

4 tbsp lemon dressing

a few fresh nasturtium flowers
 (optional)

NUTRITION FACTS	
Amount per Serving	
Calories 81	Calories from Fat 36
	% Daily Value
Total Fat 4g	6%
Saturated Fat 0.4g	2%
Polyunsaturated Fat 2.5g	0%
Monounsaturated Fat 1g	0%
Cholesterol 0mg	0%
Sodium 160mg	7%
Total Carbohydrate 6g	2%
Dietary Fibre 4g	16%
Sugars 6g	0%
Protein 4g	0%

Percent daily values are based on a 2000 calorie diet

≈ Remove and discard any coarse stems from the spinach and tear the leaves into pieces. Place in a colander to drain well. Place the pine nuts in a small, dry pan over medium-high heat, and roast until lightly browned, stirring all the time. Remove from the pan and leave to cool.

≈ Wash the figs, trim off the stems, cut each into quarters and then into thin slices. Place the spinach, pine nuts and figs in a serving bowl. Sprinkle the dressing over the mixture, toss well, and garnish with a few fresh nasturtium flowers, if available.

BAKED SALAD OF RED PEPPERS AND TOMATO

SERVES 4

The name of this recipe is asadilla, *meaning "little baked vegetables" and this all-red salad is a summer favourite. It can be served with lightly toasted bread or decorated with anchovy strips.*

2 large red peppers

2 beefsteak tomatoes

3 tbsp olive oil

2 garlic cloves, finely chopped

1 tbsp chopped fresh oregano

salt and freshly ground black pepper

NUTRITION FACTS	
Amount per Serving	
Calories 117	Calories from Fat 80
	% Daily Value
Total Fat 9g	14%
Saturated Fat 1.5g	7.5%
Polyunsaturated Fat 1g	0%
Monounsaturated Fat 6g	0%
Cholesterol 0mg	0%
Sodium 10mg	0.4%
Total Carbohydrate 8g	3%
Dietary Fibre 3g	12%
Sugars 8g	0%
Protein 1.5g	0%

Percent daily values are based on a 2000 calorie diet

≈ Skin the peppers. Hold them on a carving fork over a gas flame, until black and blistered. (Alternatively grill, giving them a quarter turn every 5 minutes.) Put them in a plastic bag for 10 minutes. Then strip off the skins. Pull out the stems and discard the seeds but reserve the juice.

≈ Meanwhile, skin the tomatoes, quarter them, remove seeds and juice (reserving it for later). Slice the tomato flesh lengthways into strips and put into an oiled baking dish.

≈ Slice the peppers the same way and mix in. Sprinkle with the garlic, herbs, remaining oil and salt and pepper. Press the tomato and pepper juices through a sieve, add them and mix everything gently. Bake in a preheated oven (at the highest temperature possible) for about 20 minutes then leave until cold.

≈ This is delicious as a salad, but it can also be puréed to make a sauce for other dishes. Because it stores well in a screw-top jar in the refrigerator (for a week or more), it is worth doubling and trebling quantities.

LAYERED TOMATO AND PASTA SALAD

SERVES 8

This is a good recipe to remember when you are on holiday in a Mediterranean country, where there are ripe tomatoes bursting with flavour and wonderfully satisfying close-textured bread to mop up the juices.

225 g/8 oz bowtie pasta

salt and freshly ground black pepper

1 kg/2¼ lb tomatoes, peeled and
    sliced

a little balsamic or cider vinegar

3 garlic cloves, finely chopped

about 12 black olives, thinly sliced

handful of sprigs of basil, shredded

good-quality virgin olive oil

croûtons, to serve

≈ Cook the pasta in boiling salted water for about 15 minutes, or according to the instructions on the package, until tender. While the pasta is cooking, sprinkle the tomatoes with salt and a little vinegar (do not be too generous with the vinegar, a few drops from the cap of the bottle will do).

≈ Drain the pasta, and layer it, while hot, with the tomatoes in a serving dish.

Sprinkle each layer of tomatoes with garlic, freshly ground black pepper, olives and basil. Then pour a little olive oil over the top (not as much as you would add to a salad), and cover the dish. Marinate for 2–3 hours before serving.

≈ To serve, pour a little more oil over the salad, and sprinkle with croutons.

NUTRITION FACTS	
Amount per Serving	
Calories 205	Calories from Fat 45
	% Daily Value
Total Fat 5g	8%
Saturated Fat 1g	5%
Polyunsaturated Fat 1g	0%
Monounsaturated Fat 2g	0%
Cholesterol 0mg	0%
Sodium 176mg	7%
Total Carbohydrate 37g	12%
Dietary Fibre 5g	20%
Sugars 7g	0%
Protein 6g	0%

Percent daily values are based on a 2000 calorie diet

SHREDDED VEGETABLE AND LINGUINE SALAD

SERVES 4

This is the ideal accompaniment for all kinds of dishes. Remember this recipe next time you plan a barbecue; it will make a complete meal with other vegetable dishes, such as kababs.

225 g/8 oz coarsely grated, baby
    carrots
salt and freshly ground black pepper
juice of 1 orange
1 tbsp hazelnut or walnut oil
225 g/8 oz courgettes, coarsely
    grated
juice of 1 lime
3 tbsp olive oil
4 sprigs of basil, shredded
350 g/12 oz fresh linguine
    (flat spaghetti)
6 spring onions, finely chopped

Garnish
sprigs of basil

≈ Mix the carrots with a little salt and pepper. Toss with the orange juice and hazelnut or walnut oil; then marinate for at least an hour before serving.

≈ Toss the courgettes with the lime juice, 1 tablespoon of the olive oil, and the basil. Cover, and let sit for 30 minutes or so (the courgettes should not marinate for as long as the carrots).

≈ Cook the linguine in plenty of boiling salted water for 3 minutes, or until tender. Drain well, and toss with the remaining olive oil, spring onions and plenty of pepper.

≈ Layer the pasta, carrots, and courgettes in a serving dish, or arrange them on a large platter or shallow dish.

Garnish with basil, and serve immediately.

NUTRITION FACTS	
Amount per Serving	
Calories 431	Calories from Fat 117
	% Daily Value
Total Fat 13g	20%
Saturated Fat 2g	10%
Polyunsaturated Fat 4g	0%
Monounsaturated Fat 7g	0%
Cholesterol 0mg	0%
Sodium 25mg	1%
Total Carbohydrate 70g	3%
Dietary Fibre 6g	24%
Sugars 8g	0%
Protein 12g	0%

Percent daily values are based on a 2000 calorie diet

PASTA SALAD WITH FRESH DATES

SERVES 4

225 g/8 oz pasta shapes (such as oricchietti)

salt and freshly ground black pepper

4 celery sticks, sliced

1 tbsp pine nuts

50 g/2 oz roughly chopped walnuts or pecan nuts

225 g/8 oz fresh dates, pitted and sliced

1 bunch of watercress

4 tbsp chopped parsley

1 tbsp chopped mint

handful of fresh basil leaves, shredded

3 tbsp balsamic vinegar

1 garlic clove, crushed and chopped

1 tbsp walnut oil

125 ml/4 fl oz olive oil

NUTRITION FACTS	
Amount per Serving	
Calories 650	Calories from Fat 378
	% Daily Value
Total Fat 42g	65%
Saturated Fat 5g	25%
Polyunsaturated Fat 12g	0%
Monounsaturated Fat 23g	0%
Cholesterol 0mg	0%
Sodium 40mg	2%
Total Carbohydrate 61g	20%
Dietary Fibre 6g	24%
Sugars 20g	0%
Protein 11g	0%

Percent daily values are based on a 2000 calorie diet

≈ Cook the pasta in boiling salted water for about 15 minutes, or according to the instructions on the package, until tender.

≈ Blanch the celery in boiling salted water for 1 minute; then drain.

≈ Dry-roast the pine nuts in a small, heavy saucepan over a low to medium heat, and shake it often or stir, so that the nuts brown lightly and evenly.

≈ Mix the walnuts or pecans, pine nuts, dates, watercress, parsley, mint and basil in a large bowl.

≈ Whisk the balsamic vinegar, garlic, and salt and pepper to taste in a bowl; then slowly whisk in the walnut and olive oils. Pour the dressing over the nut and date mixture.

≈ Drain the cooked pasta, and add it to the bowl; toss well, and cover until cooled before serving.

YOGURT WITH PASSION FRUIT

Serves 2

A refreshing snack that is quick to prepare and nutritious.

225 ml/8 fl oz yogurt
2–3 passion fruit
100 g/4 oz cashew nuts
sugar to taste (optional)
4 lettuce leaves

Garnish
cucumber

≈ Place the yogurt in a bowl. Halve the passion fruit and stir in the nuts. Add sugar, if desired.

≈ Spoon the mixture into a serving dish lined with 4 lettuce leaves garnished with cucumber and serve with warm brown rolls.

NUTRITION FACTS	
Amount per Serving	
Calories 123	Calories from Fat 63
	% Daily Value
Total Fat 7g	11%
Saturated Fat 2g	10%
Polyunsaturated Fat 1g	0%
Monounsaturated Fat 4g	0%
Cholesterol 3mg	1%
Sodium 67mg	3%
Total Carbohydrate 9g	3%
Dietary Fibre 1g	4%
Sugars 7g	0%
Protein 7g	0%

Percent daily values are based on a 2000 calorie diet

HERBED MUSHROOM PASTA SALAD

SERVES 4

Any small pasta shapes would be suitable for this dish. It can be served as a filling main course at lunchtime, or as an accompaniment.

450 g/1 lb dried pasta shapes

dash of olive oil

50 g/2 oz mushrooms, quartered

1 red pepper, seeded and cut into small squares

1 yellow pepper, seeded and cut into small squares

1 cup pitted black olives

4 tbsp chopped, fresh basil

2 tbsp chopped, fresh parsley

Dressing

2 tsp red wine vinegar

1 tsp salt

freshly ground black pepper

4 tbsp extra virgin olive oil

1 clove of garlic, crushed

1–2 tsp Dijon mustard

NUTRITION FACTS	
Amount per Serving	
Calories 566	Calories from Fat 162
	% Daily Value
Total Fat 18g	28%
Saturated Fat 3g	15%
Polyunsaturated Fat 2.5g	0%
Monounsaturated Fat 10.5g	0%
Cholesterol 0mg	0%
Sodium 620mg	26%
Total Carbohydrate 91g	30%
Dietary Fibre 9g	36%
Sugars 8g	0%
Protein 16g	0%

Percent daily values are based on a 2000 calorie diet

≈ Bring a large saucepan of water to a boil, and add the pasta shapes with a dash of olive oil. Cook for about 10 minutes, stirring occasionally, until tender. Drain, and rinse under cold running water. Drain well again.

≈ Place the cooked pasta shapes in a large salad bowl, and add the remaining salad ingredients. Mix well.

≈ To make the dressing, place all the ingredients in a screw-top jar and shake well. Pour the dressing on top of the salad and toss.

≈ Cover and refrigerate for at least 30 minutes, then toss again before serving.

STUFFED PASTA SHELLS

SERVES 4

These are great as an appetizer or served as a canapé at a party. They can be made in advance and served cold, or reheated in the oven to serve warm.

≈ Bring a large saucepan of water to the boil, and add the shells and a dash of olive oil. Cook for about 10 minutes, stirring occasionally, until tender. Drain, and rinse under cold running water. Drain again, and lay out on paper towels.

≈ To make the filling, bring a large saucepan of water to a boil and add the lentils. Simmer for about 30 minutes, until tender. Drain, and rinse under boiling water.

≈ Place the garlic, chopped tomatoes, tomato paste, fresh basil, wine, and salt and freshly ground black pepper in a large frying pan. Bring to a boil, then reduce the heat and simmer for 2–3 minutes. Add the lentils, stir, and cook for about 10 minutes, until the moisture has evaporated and the mixture has thickened.

≈ Use a teaspoon to stuff the pasta shells with the filling mixture; arrange shells on a baking sheet. Combine the topping ingredients in a small bowl, and sprinkle over the stuffed shells. Place under a hot grill for about 5 minutes, until golden.

350 g/12oz dried conchiglie rigate (large shells)

dash of olive oil

Filling

175 g/6 oz brown lentils, washed and drained

2 cloves of garlic, crushed

350 g/14-oz can chopped tomatoes

1 tbsp tomato paste

3 tbsp chopped, fresh basil

4 tbsp dry red wine

salt and freshly ground black pepper

Topping

4 tbsp fine dried breadcrumbs

50 g/2 oz finely grated fresh Parmesan cheese

3 tbsp chopped fresh parsley

NUTRITION FACTS	
Amount per Serving	
Calories 461	Calories from Fat 63
	% Daily Value
Total Fat 7g	11%
Saturated Fat 2.5g	12.5%
Polyunsaturated Fat 1g	0%
Monounsaturated Fat 2g	0%
Cholesterol 10mg	3%
Sodium 280mg	12%
Total Carbohydrate 77g	26%
Dietary Fibre 11g	44%
Sugars 5g	0%
Protein 26g	0%

Percent daily values are based on a 2000 calorie diet

DIPS, SALSAS, RELISHES AND SAUCES

YOGURT, CUCUMBER AND GARLIC DIP

SERVES 4

This light and refreshing dip should always be served well chilled. It is very easy to make, and delicious on its own with fresh pitta bread or as an accompaniment to fritters and other fried foods.

450 ml/16 fl oz natural yogurt

½ cucumber

3 garlic cloves, crushed

2 tbsp chopped fresh mint

2 tbsp olive oil

1 tbsp white-wine vinegar

salt, to taste

Garnish

chopped fresh mint

≈ Place the yogurt in a medium-sized bowl. Peel and grate the cucumber, squeezing a little at a time in the palm of your hand to remove the excess water. Stir the cucumber into the yogurt.

≈ Stir in the garlic, fresh mint, olive oil and vinegar; season with salt, to taste. Cover and chill in the refrigerator until required. Just before serving, garnish with chopped fresh mint.

NUTRITION FACTS	
Amount per Serving	
Calories 125	Calories from Fat 60
	% Daily Value
Total Fat 6.5g	10%
Saturated Fat 1g	5%
Polyunsaturated Fat 0.5g	0%
Monounsaturated Fat 4g	0%
Cholesterol 5mg	2%
Sodium 96mg	4%
Total Carbohydrate 10g	3%
Dietary Fibre 1g	4%
Sugars 10g	0%
Protein 7g	0%

Percent daily values are based on a 2000 calorie diet

STARFRUIT AND BLACK BEAN SALSA

SERVES 6

This salsa is an unusual accompaniment for grilled dishes.

225 g/8-oz can black beans, drained

140 g/5 oz corn kernels, fresh, frozen, or canned and drained

225 g/8 oz ripe tomatoes, chopped

4 spring onions, trimmed and chopped

½ green pepper, seeded and finely diced

½ red pepper, seeded and finely diced

2 tbsp olive oil

110 ml/4 fl oz red-wine vinegar

chilli sauce to taste

ground cumin to taste

salt and freshly ground black pepper to taste

1 starfruit, ½ sliced crosswise in thin sections, ½ diced

≈ Mix the beans with the corn, tomatoes, onions, peppers, olive oil and vinegar; season to taste with the chilli sauce, Worcestershire sauce, cumin, and salt and pepper. Stir diced starfruit slices into the mixture and place the other slices across the top.

≈ Cover and refrigerate at least 3 hours to allow the flavours to blend, then serve chilled.

NUTRITION FACTS	
Amount per Serving	
Calories 128	Calories from Fat 45
	% Daily Value
Total Fat 5g	8%
Saturated Fat 1g	5%
Polyunsaturated Fat 1g	0%
Monounsaturated Fat 3g	0%
Cholesterol 0mg	0%
Sodium 110mg	5%
Total Carbohydrate 17g	6%
Dietary Fibre 4g	16%
Sugars 6g	0%
Protein 5g	0%

Percent daily values are based on a 2000 calorie diet

PINEAPPLE-COCONUT RELISH

SERVES 6

225 g/8 oz diced ripe pineapple

110 g/4 oz seeded and diced yellow
pepper

½ diced red onion

1 diced chilli pepper

110 g/4 oz unsweetened shredded
dry coconut

1 tbsp sherry vinegar

≈ Combine all ingredients in bowl.

≈ Cover and let stand at room
temperature for at least 10–15 minutes
until ready to serve.

NUTRITION FACTS	
Amount per Serving	
Calories 62	Calories from Fat 45
	% Daily Value
Total Fat 5g	8%
Saturated Fat 4.5g	22%
Polyunsaturated Fat 0.2g	0%
Monounsaturated Fat 0.3g	0%
Cholesterol 0mg	0%
Sodium 3mg	0.1%
Total Carbohydrate 3g	1%
Dietary Fibre 2g	8%
Sugars 3g	0%
Protein 1g	0%

Percent daily values are based on a 2000 calorie diet

GUACAMOLE

SERVES 4

When you make guacamole, make plenty: it is so delicious that a couple of mouthfuls is more tantalizing than satisfying. The recipe below is (just) enough for four; serve with corn chips.

½ dried chilli pepper

1 clove garlic

2 large or 4 small avocados, very ripe

≈ Seed and shred the chilli pepper; pound in a mortar with the garlic and 1–2 tbsp of water. Leave for 5–10 minutes. Mash the avocado with a potato masher. Mix in the chilli pepper-garlic paste, strained through a tea-strainer.

≈ This is good for a dip; for a garnish, you can double the amounts of garlic and pepper.

NUTRITION FACTS	
Amount per Serving	
Calories 138	Calories from Fat 126
	% Daily Value
Total Fat 14g	21%
Saturated Fat 3g	15%
Polyunsaturated Fat 2g	0%
Monounsaturated Fat 9g	0%
Cholesterol 0mg	0%
Sodium 4mg	0.2%
Total Carbohydrate 1.5g	0.5%
Dietary Fibre 4g	16%
Sugars 0.4g	0%
Protein 1g	0%

Percent daily values are based on a 2000 calorie diet

FANCY GUACAMOLE

SERVES 4

basic ingredients, as for guacamole

1 medium tomato

½ small onion

1 tbsp chopped coriander

salt

≈ Peel, seed, and finely chop the tomato. Chop the onion finely in a food processor. Add these ingredients to the guacamole. Salt if desired.

≈ For further variations, omit the red pepper or the garlic or both, and add one finely chopped serrano chilli. You may also wish to add chopped coriander. None of this will necessarily make a better guacamole, just a different one.

NUTRITION FACTS	
Amount per Serving	
Calories 146	Calories from Fat 126
	% Daily Value
Total Fat 14g	21.5%
Saturated Fat 3g	15%
Polyunsaturated Fat 2g	0%
Monounsaturated Fat 9g	0%
Cholesterol 0mg	0%
Sodium 7mg	0.3%
Total Carbohydrate 3g	1%
Dietary Fibre 4g	16%
Sugars 1.5g	0%
Protein 2g	0%

Percent daily values are based on a 2000 calorie diet

PINEAPPLE SALSA

SERVES 6

450 g/16 oz peeled and cored fresh
    ripe pineapple, or canned crushed
    pineapple in its own juice

3 tbsp chopped fresh coriander

2 tsp fresh-squeezed lime juice

⅛ tsp ground cumin

⅛ tsp fresh-ground white pepper

≈ In a medium bowl, combine all ingredients, cover and refrigerate. Serve chilled.

NUTRITION FACTS	
Amount per Serving	
Calories 14	Calories from Fat 0
	% Daily Value
Total Fat 0g	0%
Saturated Fat 0g	0%
Polyunsaturated Fat 0g	0%
Monounsaturated Fat 0g	0%
Cholesterol 0mg	0%
Sodium 1mg	0%
Total Carbohydrate 3g	1%
Dietary Fibre 0.5g	2%
Sugars 3g	0%
Protein 0.2g	0%

Percent daily values are based on a 2000 calorie diet

TOMATO PEPPER SALSA (*SOFRITO*)

SERVES 6

Sofrito comes from the Spanish verb meaning "to sauté." This thick tomato-pepper salsa is a staple in many Mediterranean kitchens. It complements rice dishes and omelettes, or use it to spread on tortillas.

2 onions, finely chopped

1 large green pepper, seeded and diced

5 cloves garlic, mashed

110 ml/4 fl oz olive oil

110 g/4-oz jar diced pimentos, drained

225 g/8-oz can tomato sauce

1 tsp dried oregano

1 tbsp red-wine vinegar

≈ In a large skillet, over low heat, sauté onions, green pepper and garlic in the olive oil for about 15 minutes until tender and lightly browned. Add pimentos and cook 5 more minutes over low heat.

≈ Add tomato sauce, oregano and vinegar and cook 10 more minutes. Let cool, then store in tightly closed jar in the refrigerator up to 2 weeks.

NUTRITION FACTS	
Amount per Serving	
Calories 191	Calories from Fat 162
	% Daily Value
Total Fat 18g	28%
Saturated Fat 3g	15%
Polyunsaturated Fat 2g	0%
Monounsaturated Fat 13g	0%
Cholesterol 0mg	0%
Sodium 31mg	1%
Total Carbohydrate 5g	2%
Dietary Fibre 2g	8%
Sugars 4g	0%
Protein 1g	0%

Percent daily values are based on a 2000 calorie diet

1½ tsp grated lime zest

50 ml/2 fl oz lime juice

4 tbsp curry powder

110 ml/4 fl oz safflower oil

salt and freshly ground black pepper to taste

paw-paw seeds to taste (optional)

NUTRITION FACTS	
Amount per Serving	
Calories 169	Calories from Fat 162
	% Daily Value
Total Fat 18g	28%
Saturated Fat 2g	10%
Polyunsaturated Fat 13g	0%
Monounsaturated Fat 2g	0%
Cholesterol 0mg	0%
Sodium 10mg	0.4%
Total Carbohydrate 1g	0.3%
Dietary Fibre 1g	4%
Sugars 0.1g	0%
Protein 0.2g	0%

Percent daily values are based on a 2000 calorie diet

½ tsp salt

1 clove garlic, minced

1 small chilli pepper, seeded and minced

50 ml/2 fl oz lime juice

100 ml/3 fl oz minced onion

6 tbsp cold water

1–2 tbsp chopped fresh coriander (optional)

NUTRITION FACTS	
Amount per Serving	
Calories 5	Calories from Fat 0
	% Daily Value
Total Fat 0g	0%
Saturated Fat 0g	0%
Polyunsaturated Fat 0g	0%
Monounsaturated Fat 0g	0%
Cholesterol 0mg	0%
Sodium 1mg	0%
Total Carbohydrate 1g	0.3%
Dietary Fibre 0.2g	0.8%
Sugars 1g	0%
Protein 0.2g	0%

Percent daily values are based on a 2000 calorie diet

CURRY-LIME VINAIGRETTE

SERVES 6

A delicious complement to artichokes, mushrooms and asparagus, this vinaigrette substitutes refreshing lime for the usual lemon.

≈ In a medium bowl, combine zest and lime juice. Whisk in curry powder, safflower oil and desired seasoning. Stir well and serve at room temperature.

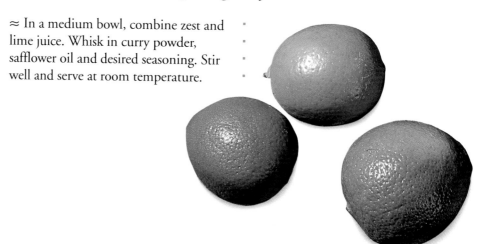

PEPPER-LIME DIP

SERVES 6

This dip complements many vegetable dishes but is especially good with artichokes.

≈ Mash salt with garlic and chilli pepper to form a paste. Stir in lime juice, onion, water and coriander, if desired.

≈ Let stand 1 hour before serving.

SAVOURY KUMQUAT SAUCE

MAKES 550 ML/1 PT

This is a savoury, orange-type sauce to serve with all kinds of vegetable dishes.

2 spring onions, trimmed and sliced

1 tsp freshly grated ginger

peel of 1 lime, thinly cut into strips

110 g/4 oz kumquats, cut into
    quarters with seeds removed

½ vegetable bouillon cube

550 ml/1 pt water

finely grated peel and juice of
    1 orange

3 tbsp cornflour

2 tbsp sugar

NUTRITION FACTS	
Amount per Serving (550 ml)	
Calories 429	Calories from Fat 9
	% Daily Value
Total Fat 1g	1.5%
Saturated Fat 0.1g	0.5%
Polyunsaturated Fat 0.2g	0%
Monounsaturated Fat 0.1g	0%
Cholesterol 0mg	0%
Sodium 41mg	2%
Total Carbohydrate 110g	37%
Dietary Fibre 5g	20%
Sugars 55g	0%
Protein 2g	0%

Percent daily values are based on a 2000 calorie diet

≈ Put the onions, ginger, lime, kumquats, bouillon cube and water into a saucepan and cook for about 10–15 minutes until the kumquats are soft.

≈ Blend the orange juice and peel with the cornflour and stir into the kumquat mixture. Bring slowly to a boil, stirring, and cook for 2–3 minutes until thickened and clear. Add sugar to taste.

PAW-PAW-MANGO SALSA

SERVES 6

≈ Peel, seed the paw-paw and mango, and cut into bite sized pieces. Seed and mince the jalapeño pepper.

≈ In a medium bowl, combine with all the remaining ingredients, cover and refrigerate. Serve chilled.

½ paw-paw
½ mango
1 fresh jalapeño pepper
1 spring onion, chopped
1 tbsp sugar
1 tbsp chopped fresh coriander
1 tbsp finely chopped red pepper
paw-paw seeds to taste (optional)

NUTRITION FACTS	
Amount per Serving	
Calories 29	Calories from Fat 0
	% Daily Value
Total Fat 0g	0%
Saturated Fat 0g	0%
Polyunsaturated Fat 0g	0%
Monounsaturated Fat 0g	0%
Cholesterol 0mg	0%
Sodium 8mg	0.3%
Total Carbohydrate 7g	2%
Dietary Fibre 2g	8%
Sugars 5g	0%
Protein 0.3g	0%

Percent daily values are based on a 2000 calorie diet

MANGO AND GREEN TOMATO CHUTNEY

MAKES APPROXIMATELY 1.8 KG/4 LB

900 g/2 lb mangoes, peeled and
  quartered

675 mg/1½ lb tart apples, peeled and
  chopped

1 onion, chopped

450 g/1 lb green tomatoes, chopped

160 g/6 oz raisins

juice of 1 large lemon

560 ml/1 pt vinegar

2 tbsp salt

¼ tsp cayenne pepper

¼ tsp nutmeg

3 bay leaves

1½ tbsp lime juice

900 g/2 lb brown sugar

≈ Place all the ingredients except the lime juice and sugar in a large bowl, mix thoroughly and leave to stand for at least 3 hours.

≈ Transfer to a preserving pan, bring to the boil and simmer gently until tender, stirring frequently.

≈ Add the lime juice and sugar and stir until the sugar is dissolved. Continue to simmer until thick and of the desired consistency.

≈ Pour into warmed jars, cover and label.

NUTRITION FACTS	
Amount (makes approx. 1.8 kg)	
Calories 4348	Calories from Fat 40
	% Daily Value
Total Fat 4.5g	7%
Saturated Fat 1g	5%
Polyunsaturated Fat 2g	0%
Monounsaturated Fat 0.5g	0%
Cholesterol 0mg	0%
Sodium 640mg	27%
Total Carbohydrate 1140g	38%
Dietary Fibre 58g	232%
Sugars 1086g	0%
Protein 16g	0%

Percent daily values are based on a 2000 calorie diet

PAW-PAW AND ORANGE RELISH

MAKES APPROXIMATELY **900 G/2 LB**

≈ Place the onions, garlic, cider vinegar and ginger in a saucepan and cook for 10 minutes to slightly soften the onion.

≈ Halve the paw-paw, scoop out the seeds, and peel. Cut the flesh into small dice, and add to the remaining ingredients in the pan.

≈ Cook for about 15 minutes until the paw-paw is just cooked and still retains its shape. Remove the orange peel and whole spices, if desired. Remove the ginger and chilli peppers unless a hot relish is preferred. Pot into jars while still hot.

2 onions, chopped

3 small cloves garlic, crushed

225 ml/½ pt cider vinegar

4 cm/1½ in fresh ginger, sliced

2 medium-sized paw-paw (approx 675 g/1½ lb)

peel and juice of 1 orange

6 cloves garlic

3 dried chilli peppers

6 allspice berries

½ tsp salt

75 g/3 oz light soft brown sugar

110 g/4 oz seeded raisins, chopped

NUTRITION FACTS	
Amount per Serving (900 g)	
Calories 784	Calories from Fat 18
	% Daily Value
Total Fat 2g	3%
Saturated Fat 0.2g	1%
Polyunsaturated Fat 0.2g	0%
Monounsaturated Fat 0g	0%
Cholesterol 0mg	0%
Sodium 115mg	5%
Total Carbohydrate 188g	63%
Dietary Fibre 22g	88%
Sugars 182g	0%
Protein 8.5g	0%

Percent daily values are based on a 2000 calorie diet

STRAWBERRY AND KIWI FRUIT RELISH

MAKES 280 ML/½ PT

This recipe could be made with low-fat yogurt instead of low-fat mayonnaise, depending on the accompanying dishes and personal preference. Serve chilled.

dash each of salt and freshly ground
    black pepper
1 tsp sugar
½ tsp Dijon mustard
2 tbsp light oil
1 tbsp tarragon vinegar
3 tbsp low fat mayonnaise
2 tsp chopped fresh tarragon
350 g/12 oz strawberries, sliced
1 kiwi fruit, peeled and quartered

≈ Place the seasoning, sugar and mustard in a bowl, stir in the oil and gradually beat in the vinegar, mayonnaise and tarragon. Add the strawberries and the kiwi fruit. Chill and serve.

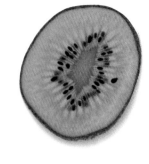

NUTRITION FACTS	
Amount per Serving (280 ml)	
Calories 534	Calories from Fat 400
	% Daily Value
Total Fat 44g	68%
Saturated Fat 3g	15%
Polyunsaturated Fat 14g	0%
Monounsaturated Fat 5g	0%
Cholesterol 17mg	6%
Sodium 780mg	32%
Total Carbohydrate 32g	11%
Dietary Fibre 5g	20%
Sugars 29g	0%
Protein 3g	0%

Percent daily values are based on a 2000 calorie diet

BANANA RELISH

MAKES 170 ML/6 FL OZ

Serve this relish with barbecued food.

1 tbsp olive oil
1 small onion, finely chopped
2 tsp grainy mustard
1 tsp sugar
4 medium-sized bananas, peeled
2 tsp white malt-vinegar

≈ Melt the oil and fry the onion slowly, without browning, until soft. Stir in the mustard and sugar and cook for 1 minute.

≈ Mash the bananas and add the remaining ingredients. Cook for 2–3 minutes to soften the banana. Serve at room temperature.

NUTRITION FACTS	
Amount per Serving (170 ml)	
Calories 588	Calories from Fat 110
	% Daily Value
Total Fat 12.5g	19%
Saturated Fat 2g	10%
Polyunsaturated Fat 1g	0%
Monounsaturated Fat 8g	0%
Cholesterol 0mg	0%
Sodium 126mg	5%
Total Carbohydrate 120g	40%
Dietary Fibre 7g	28%
Sugars 109g	0%
Protein 6g	0%

Percent daily values are based on a 2000 calorie diet

LEMON FENNEL SAUCE

MAKES 300 ML/½ PT

This is a sharp, tangy pouring sauce.

3 tbsp olive oil

1 bulb fresh fennel, finely chopped

2 tsp flour

grated peel of 1 lemon

juice of 2 lemons

150 ml/5 fl oz water

1 tbsp fresh fennel leaves, chopped

1 tsp sugar

salt and freshly ground black pepper

NUTRITION FACTS	
Amount per Serving (300 ml)	
Calories 485	Calories from Fat 306
	% Daily Value
Total Fat 34g	52%
Saturated Fat 5g	25%
Polyunsaturated Fat 3g	0%
Monounsaturated Fat 24g	0%
Cholesterol 0mg	0%
Sodium 26mg	1%
Total Carbohydrate 42g	14%
Dietary Fibre 9g	36%
Sugars 11g	0%
Protein 6g	0%

Percent daily values are based on a 2000 calorie diet

≈ Heat the oil in a saucepan, add the chopped fennel and stir. Cover and cook gently for 5 minutes to soften.

≈ Add the flour and cook for 30 seconds, then stir in the lemon peel and juice, together with the water. Bring to the boil and cook for a further 2 minutes until thickened. Add the fennel leaves and sugar, if required. Season to taste.

PLUM AND RED WINE SAUCE

SERVES 4

Serve this sauce with ice cream or cheesecake.

225 g/½ lb red plums

230 ml/8 fl oz plus 2 tbsp water

115 g/4 oz sugar

125 ml/4 fl oz red wine

2 tsp arrowroot

2 tbsp water

≈ Wash the plums, halve them and remove the stones. Place the plums, water and sugar in a saucepan, heat and stir to dissolve the sugar. Add the wine and cook until the plums are soft. Purée the plums in a blender and return to the saucepan.

≈ Blend the arrowroot with 2 tbsp water and stir into the purée. Bring to the boil, stirring, until thickened and clear. If the sauce appears too thick, add a little extra water or orange juice.

NUTRITION FACTS	
Amount per Serving	
Calories 261	Calories from Fat 0
	% Daily Value
Total Fat 0g	0%
Saturated Fat 0g	0%
Polyunsaturated Fat 0g	0%
Monounsaturated Fat 0g	0%
Cholesterol 0mg	0%
Sodium 6mg	0.3%
Total Carbohydrate 64g	21%
Dietary Fibre 1g	4%
Sugars 61g	0%
Protein 0.5g	0%

Percent daily values are based on a 2000 calorie diet

ONION PURÉE

MAKES ABOUT 450 G/1 LB

4 tsp olive oil

675 g/1½ lb onions, finely chopped

salt and pepper

3 garlic cloves

NUTRITION FACTS

Amount per Serving (450 g)

Calories 324   Calories from Fat 145

	% Daily Value
Total Fat 16g	25%
Saturated Fat 2g	10%
Polyunsaturated Fat 2g	0%
Monounsaturated Fat 11g	0%
Cholesterol 0mg	0%
Sodium 15mg	0.6%
Total Carbohydrate 41g	14%
Dietary Fibre 1.5g	6%
Sugars 28g	0%
Protein 7g	0%

Percent daily values are based on a 2000 calorie diet

This gently stewed mixture of onions and oil is the basis of many Mediterranean dishes and sauces. It can be made in advance and stored for several days in the refrigerator.

≈ Heat the oil in a heavy pan that has a lid. Stir in the onions, add salt, cover, and cook over a very low heat for about 1 hour, until the onions have softened and almost disintegrated.

≈ Add the garlic cloves, stir and increase the heat slightly. Leave to cook until the onions are an even brown. Remove the garlic, if preferred, and season to taste.

RED PEPPER PASTE

MAKES ABOUT 300 ML/½ PT

3 large red peppers, seeded and
    quartered lengthwise

1 tbsp sea salt

2 garlic cloves

4 tbsp olive oil

NUTRITION FACTS

Amount per Serving (300 ml)

Calories 574   Calories from Fat 415

	% Daily Value
Total Fat 46g	71%
Saturated Fat 7g	35%
Polyunsaturated Fat 5g	0%
Monounsaturated Fat 32g	0%
Cholesterol 0mg	0%
Sodium 22mg	1%
Total Carbohydrate 36g	12%
Dietary Fibre 12g	48%
Sugars 33g	0%
Protein 6g	0%

Percent daily values are based on a 2000 calorie diet

A paste of roasted red peppers has now become a fashionable ingredient, but it has been used in the Mediterranean countries for many years as a flavouring for grills and marinades. The garlic cloves can also be roasted, before peeling, if liked. The paste can be kept in a covered glass jar in the refrigerator for 2 weeks.

≈ Stir together the peppers and salt; then leave, uncovered, at room temperature for 24 hours.

≈ Preheat the grill. Rinse the peppers well, drain and pat dry. Place, skin side up, on a baking sheet. Grill until the skins are charred and blistered. Leave to cool slightly before peeling off the skins and discarding.

≈ Purée the garlic and peppers in a blender, pouring in the oil slowly.

PIRI-PIRI CHILLI SAUCE

MAKES ABOUT 5 TBSP

This is a chilli-based sauce that provides the fire in many savoury dishes – it is easier to add a few drops of the ready-made chilli-based sauce than to seed and chop chilli peppers each time. Like other traditional recipes, nearly everyone who makes Piri-piri has their own version, the simplest of which is to fill a third of a jar or bottle with small, red chilli peppers, then top up with olive oil, cover and leave in a cool place for at least 1 month so the oil is impregnated with their heat. Other versions, like the one below, include lemon juice or vinegar. Hot pepper sauce can be substituted.

½ small red pepper

4–5 fresh red chilli peppers

juice of 1½ lemons

2 tsp olive oil

salt

≈ De-seed and slice the pepper and red chilli peppers.

≈ Simmer the red pepper and chilli peppers in a saucepan with the lemon juice for about 15 minutes until tender.

≈ Place in a blender with the oil and mix until thick. Season with salt. Pour into a small bottle or jar, cover and keep in a cool place.

NUTRITION FACTS	
Amount per Serving (1 tbsp)	
Calories 24	Calories from Fat 13
	% Daily Value
Total Fat 1.5g	2%
Saturated Fat 0.2g	1%
Polyunsaturated Fat 0.2g	0%
Monounsaturated Fat 1g	0%
Cholesterol 0mg	0%
Sodium 2mg	0%
Total Carbohydrate 2g	0.6%
Dietary Fibre 1g	4%
Sugars 2g	0%
Protein 0.4g	0%

Percent daily values are based on a 2000 calorie diet

TOMATO SAUCE

MAKES ABOUT 600 ML/1 PT

Tomato sauce is a staple for Mediterranean cooks. The special taste is not only because the tomatoes from this region are sweet and richly flavoured, but because of the amount of oil that is used, so do not reduce the quantity; it emulsifies with the other ingredients when the sauce is boiled or puréed. For a greater depth of tomato flavour, add a few pieces of sun-dried tomatoes, or a little sun-dried tomato paste.

6 tbsp olive oil

2 onions, chopped

1–2 garlic cloves, chopped

2 red peppers

1 fresh red chilli pepper

1 kg/2¼ lb tomatoes, chopped

salt and pepper

≈ De-seed and slice the pepper and chilli pepper.

≈ Heat the oil, add the onion and garlic, and cook gently until they begin to soften. Stir in the peppers and chilli pepper and cook for a few minutes; then add the tomatoes and simmer, stirring occasionally, until reduced to the consistency of a sauce.

≈ Purée in a blender or food processor; then strain through a sieve to remove pieces of skin and the seeds. Season and reheat as required.

NUTRITION FACTS	
Amount per Serving (600 ml)	
Calories 929	Calories from Fat 640
	% Daily Value
Total Fat 71g	109%
Saturated Fat 11g	55%
Polyunsaturated Fat 8g	0%
Monounsaturated Fat 49g	0%
Cholesterol 0mg	0%
Sodium 110mg	4.5%
Total Carbohydrate 65g	22%
Dietary Fibre 25g	100%
Sugars 60g	0%
Protein 13g	0%

Percent daily values are based on a 2000 calorie diet

PLUM AND PUMPKIN RELISH

MAKES APPROXIMATELY 2.5 KG/5½ LB

This is a sweet and sour relish ideal for cheese. The pumpkin and onion should be slightly crisp.

900 g/2 lb piece of pumpkin

450 g/1 lb onions, sliced

300 ml/½ pt cider vinegar

6 cloves garlic, crushed

900 g/2 lb plums, halved and pitted

3 bay leaves

15 g/½ oz salt

85 g/3 oz seedless golden raisins

1 tbsp mustard seed

≈ Cut the flesh from the skin of the pumpkin and dice. Place in a large saucepan with the onions, cider vinegar and garlic. Cook slowly to just soften the pumpkin so it remains a bit crisp – about 20 minutes.

≈ Add the plums and bay leaves. Cook for a further 10–15 minutes to soften the plums without losing their shape.

≈ Remove the bay leaves. Stir in the remaining ingredients. Place in a large bowl, cover and leave for 1 week to allow the flavours to develop and the mustard seeds to swell. Stir from time to time.

≈ Store in jars.

NUTRITION FACTS	
Amount per Serving (2.5 kg)	
Calories 931	Calories from Fat 36
	% Daily Value
Total Fat 4g	6%
Saturated Fat 1g	5%
Polyunsaturated Fat 0.5g	0%
Monounsaturated Fat 0g	0%
Cholesterol 0mg	0%
Sodium 100mg	4%
Total Carbohydrate 200g	66%
Dietary Fibre 45g	180%
Sugars 182g	0%
Protein 22g	0%

Percent daily values are based on a 2000 calorie diet

MAIN DISHES

Baked Stuffed Vegetables

Baked Stuffed Courgettes

Cauliflower Baked with Tomatoes and Feta Cheese

Green Lentils with Carrot, Onion and Garlic

Stuffed Grape Leaves (*Dolmades*)

Stuffed Peppers

Spicy Okra and Mango

Spicy Stuffed Tomatoes

Spanish Baked Vegetables

Pasta-stuffed Cabbage Leaves

Aubergine Ragout

Baked Mixed Vegetables

Layered Aubergine, Potato and Tomato Casserole

Provençal Green Beans with Pasta

Fusilli with Sun-dried Tomatoes

Kidney Bean, Artichoke and Mushroom Casserole

Spaghetti with Tomatoes

Tagliatelle Neapolitan

Pasta Paella

Stuffed Squash

BAKED STUFFED VEGETABLES

SERVES 4

This recipe originated on the island of Crete, where the use of rice as the main ingredient for stuffings is most common. The addition of raisins, pine nuts or almonds makes this a truly Cretan creation.

8–10 firm, ripe vegetables, including
    tomatoes, peppers, courgettes
    and aubergine
6 tbsp olive oil
6 spring onions, finely chopped
225 g/8 oz long-grain rice
2 garlic cloves, crushed
1 tsp ground cinnamon
85 g/3 oz raisins
55 g/2 oz toasted pine nuts
salt and freshly ground black pepper,
    to taste
4 tbsp chopped fresh parsley
3 tbsp chopped fresh mint

≈ To prepare the vegetables, slice the tops off the tomatoes, peppers, courgettes and aubergine. Keep each vegetable top intact because they provide the lids for the vegetables when they are stuffed. Scoop out the seeds and flesh from the tomatoes and place in a bowl. Do the same with the aubergine and courgettes, remembering to discard the bitter seeds from the aubergine. Scoop out the seeds from the peppers and discard.

≈ In a large frying pan, heat 2 tbsp of the olive oil and add the onions. Cook for 3 minutes, then stir in the rice, garlic, cinnamon, raisins, pine nuts and the seeds and pulp reserved from the vegetables. Add enough water to cover the rice and simmer, covered, for 7–10 minutes, or until the rice is tender and the majority of the liquid has been absorbed.

≈ Stir the seasoning and herbs into the rice filling and remove from the heat. Preheat the oven to 180°C/350°F/ Gas Mark 4. Stuff the vegetables with the rice filling and place the tops on each vegetable. Arrange the vegetables in a large roasting pan and pour in enough water to just cover the base of the pan.

≈ Drizzle the remaining olive oil over the vegetables and bake for 50–60 minutes, or until the vegetables are tender. Baste the stuffed vegetables several times during cooking, but try not to rearrange them as they may break apart. Delicious served warm or cold, as desired.

NUTRITION FACTS	
Amount per Serving	
Calories 547	Calories from Fat 234
	% Daily Value
Total Fat 26g	40%
Saturated Fat 3g	30%
Polyunsaturated Fat 7g	0%
Monounsaturated Fat 14g	0%
Cholesterol 0mg	0%
Sodium 30mg	1%
Total Carbohydrate 74g	25%
Dietary Fibre 7g	28%
Sugars 19g	0%
Protein 9g	0%

Percent daily values are based on a 2000 calorie diet

BAKED STUFFED COURGETTES

SERVES 4

A delicious combination of tender courgettes and fresh coriander mixed with a sweet soy sauce. You can make the filling and the sauce a day in advance. Reheat the sauce while the courgettes are baking.

110 g/¼ lb dried vermicelli, broken into small pieces

dash of olive oil

4 medium-sized courgettes

finely chopped walnuts, to garnish

Filling

150 ml/5 fl oz soy sauce

1 clove of garlic, crushed

50 g/2 oz mushrooms, very finely chopped

3 tbsp chopped, fresh coriander

50 g/2 oz shelled walnuts, very finely chopped

salt and freshly ground black pepper

Sauce

4 tbsp olive oil

2 cloves of garlic, crushed

4 tbsp chopped, fresh coriander

salt and freshly ground black pepper

3 tbsp vegetable stock

≈ Bring a large saucepan of water to the boil, and add the vermicelli with a dash of olive oil. Cook for about 5 minutes, stirring occasionally, until tender. Drain.

≈ Cut a thin slice lengthwise along the top of each courgette, and chop this piece finely. Using a teaspoon, scoop out the flesh from the middle of the courgette and chop roughly. Arrange the hollowed courgettes in a shallow, ovenproof dish and set aside. Preheat the oven to 200°C/400°F/Gas Mark 6.

≈ To make the filling, place the sweet soy sauce and the garlic in a large frying pan and heat gently. Cook for about 1 minute, then stir in the mushrooms. Cook for about 5 minutes, stirring occasionally, then add the coriander.

Cook for a further 2–3 minutes, then stir in the chopped walnuts and season to taste with salt and freshly ground black pepper. Simmer for 1–2 minutes, then stir in the cooked vermicelli.

≈ Remove from the heat and, using a teaspoon, stuff the courgettes with the filling, placing any extra around the courgettes in the dish. Cover the dish with foil and bake for 25–30 minutes.

≈ Meanwhile, to make the sauce, place all the ingredients in a food processor or blender and purée until smooth. Transfer to a small saucepan, and heat gently until warm. Remove the stuffed courgettes from the oven. Serve with the sauce, garnished with chopped walnuts.

NUTRITION FACTS	
Amount per Serving	
Calories 322	Calories from Fat 190
	% Daily Value
Total Fat 21g	32%
Saturated Fat 3g	15%
Polyunsaturated Fat 7g	0%
Monounsaturated Fat 10g	0%
Cholesterol 0mg	0%
Sodium 5mg	0%
Total Carbohydrate 24g	8%
Dietary Fibre 3.5g	14%
Sugars 3g	0%
Protein 9g	0%

Percent daily values are based on a 2000 calorie diet

CAULIFLOWER BAKED WITH TOMATOES AND FETA CHEESE

Serves 4

This dish is enlivened with a strong flavour of tomatoes combined with the typically Greek use of ground cinnamon.

6 tbsp olive oil

1 onion, sliced

2 garlic cloves, crushed

8 tomatoes, peeled and chopped

large pinch of ground cinnamon

2 tsp dried oregano

salt and freshly ground black pepper, to taste

1 large cauliflower, cut into florets

1 tbsp freshly squeezed lemon juice

80 g/3 oz feta cheese, grated

≈ Heat 2–3 tbsp olive oil in a heavy-based pan and sauté the onion and garlic for 3–4 minutes, or until the onion has softened.

≈ Add the chopped tomatoes, cinnamon and oregano and season with salt and pepper. Stir and simmer, covered, for 5 minutes.

≈ Preheat the oven to 190°C/375°F/ Gas Mark 5. Add the cauliflower to the tomato mixture, cover, and simmer for a further 10–15 minutes or until the cauliflower is just tender. Remove from the heat.

≈ Transfer the cauliflower and tomato mixture to a large, shallow dish and drizzle over the remaining olive oil. Sprinkle over the lemon juice and grated feta. Bake for 45–50 minutes, or until the cauliflower is soft and the cheese has melted. Serve warm.

NUTRITION FACTS	
Amount per Serving	
Calories 250	Calories from Fat 190
	% Daily Value
Total Fat 21g	32%
Saturated Fat 5g	25%
Polyunsaturated Fat 2g	0%
Monounsaturated Fat 13g	0%
Cholesterol 13mg	4%
Sodium 290mg	12%
Total Carbohydrate 9g	3%
Dietary Fibre 4g	16%
Sugars 8g	0%
Protein 6.5g	0%

Percent daily values are based on a 2000 calorie diet

GREEN LENTILS WITH CARROT, ONION AND GARLIC

SERVES 6

Green lentils are recommended for this dish because the green variety will only disintegrate after extreme provocation. If you are using red lentils, cook them carefully and remove them from the heat while they are still firm and in one piece.

450 g/1 lb green lentils

4 tbsp olive oil

1 large onion

2 cloves garlic

1 medium carrot

3 tbsp flour

1 pinch each thyme, parsley, sage

salt and pepper to taste

≈ Wash the lentils thoroughly in cold water and then boil them until soft. Reserve the lentils, in their pan, until needed.

≈ While the lentils are cooking, chop the onion, crush the garlic, and slice the carrot into thin strips.

≈ In another saucepan, heat the oil over a medium heat and add the onion, the garlic and the carrot. Cook the vegetables until the onions begin to brown, then stir in the flour and cook until golden.

≈ Now lift the lentils from their cooking juices and stir them into the saucepan with the vegetables. Gradually add small amounts of the lentil stock until you have a stew the consistency of thin cream.

≈ Season to taste with the herbs, salt and pepper and serve.

NUTRITION FACTS	
Amount per Serving	
Calories 335	Calories from Fat 80
	% Daily Value
Total Fat 9g	14%
Saturated Fat 1g	5%
Polyunsaturated Fat 1g	0%
Monounsaturated Fat 6g	0%
Cholesterol 0mg	0%
Sodium 14mg	0.6%
Total Carbohydrate 47g	16%
Dietary Fibre 11g	44%
Sugars 3g	0%
Protein 20g	0%

Percent daily values are based on a 2000 calorie diet

STUFFED GRAPE LEAVES (*DOLMADES*)

SERVES 10

Use fresh grape leaves if they are available. Choose young, tender leaves of a good size. Wash and drain them well, then trim the tough stems with scissors.

30 grape leaves in brine, rinsed well

50 ml/2 fl oz olive oil

1 large onion, very finely chopped

125 g/5 oz long-grain rice

2 garlic cloves, crushed

50 g/2 oz pine nuts

50 g/2 oz seedless raisins

1 tsp ground cumin

600 ml/1 pt plus 3 tbsp water

4 tbsp chopped fresh dill

4 tbsp chopped fresh parsley

2 tbsp chopped fresh mint

salt and freshly ground black pepper, to taste

1 egg, beaten

juice of 1 lemon

≈ Fill a large saucepan with water and bring to a rolling boil. Drop the grape leaves into the water and cook for 3–5 minutes, or until softened. Drain well and set aside.

≈ Heat 2 tbsp olive oil in a large pan and sauté the onion for 3–5 minutes, or until softened. Add the rice and cook for a further 3–5 minutes, or until lightly coloured, stirring continuously with a wooden spoon.

≈ Add the garlic, pine nuts, raisins and cumin and stir in 300 ml/½ pt water. Cover and simmer for about 10 minutes, or until the rice is tender and the liquid has been absorbed. Remove from the heat and set aside to cool down.

≈ Stir the chopped fresh herbs into the rice mixture and season with salt and freshly ground black pepper. Stir in 1 tbsp of the remaining olive oil and the beaten egg.

≈ Place the remaining olive oil in a large saucepan with 3 tbsp water. Line the base of the saucepan with 3–4 grape leaves. (You can use any that are torn or otherwise imperfect for this.) To stuff the remaining grape leaves, place about 1 tsp of the rice mixture in the centre of each leaf and neatly fold the leaf around the filling to encase it completely.

≈ Place the stuffed grape leaves in the base of the saucepan, seam-sides down, and repeat with the remaining grape leaves, layering them on top of each other neatly. Sprinkle over the lemon juice and 300 ml/½ pt water. Place a plate upside-down on top of the dolmades to keep them in position during cooking. Cover with a lid and simmer for about 2 hours, or until the grape leaves are tender and the rice is cooked through.

≈ Serve warm or cold.

NUTRITION FACTS	
Amount per Serving	
Calories 129	Calories from Fat 63
	% Daily Value
Total Fat 7g	11%
Saturated Fat 1g	5%
Polyunsaturated Fat 1.5g	0%
Monounsaturated Fat 4g	0%
Cholesterol 24mg	8%
Sodium 345mg	14%
Total Carbohydrate 15g	5%
Dietary Fibre 0.5g	2%
Sugars 3.5g	0%
Protein 3g	0%

Percent daily values are based on a 2000 calorie diet

STUFFED PEPPERS

SERVES 4

225 g/½ lb small gnocchi (small dumpling shapes)

dash of olive oil

4 peppers, for stuffing

parsley sprigs, to garnish

Filling

50 ml/2 fl oz olive oil

6 spring onions, finely chopped

2 cloves of garlic, crushed

1 pepper, seeded and finely diced

salt and freshly ground black pepper

80 g/3 oz freshly grated Parmesan cheese

A refreshing alternative to rice, pasta makes a perfect filling for peppers. Tiny pasta shapes also work well in this dish. Serve with a crisp green salad.

≈ Bring a large pan of water to the boil, and add the pasta with a dash of olive oil. Cook for 10 minutes, until tender. Drain.

≈ Preheat the oven to 200°C/400°F/ Gas Mark 6. Lay each pepper on its side and slice off the top, reserving it to make the lid. Scoop out and discard the seeds and pith. Arrange the hollowed-out peppers in a shallow, ovenproof dish, and set aside.

≈ To make the filling, heat the oil and sauté the spring onions and garlic for 2 minutes, then add the diced pepper. Season with salt and pepper and cook for 5 minutes, stirring occasionally.

≈ Add the gnocchi and the Parmesan cheese to the filling mixture, and cook for about 2 minutes to heat through. Using a tablespoon, stuff each pepper with the pasta filling, scattering any extra around the edges.

≈ Place the pepper lids on each pepper and bake for about 30 minutes, until the peppers have softened. Just before serving, place under the grill for 2–3 minutes to char the pepper skins, if desired. Serve garnished with parsley sprigs.

NUTRITION FACTS

Amount per Serving

Calories 436	Calories from Fat 170
	% Daily Value
Total Fat 19g	29%
Saturated Fat 8g	40%
Polyunsaturated Fat 2g	0%
Monounsaturated Fat 8g	0%
Cholesterol 31mg	10%
Sodium 357mg	15%
Total Carbohydrate 49g	16%
Dietary Fibre 8g	32%
Sugars 7g	0%
Protein 21g	0%

Percent daily values are based on a 2000 calorie diet

SPICY OKRA AND MANGO

SERVES 4

Serve this with fairly substantial fresh pasta shapes – fresh rigatoni for example – or the dried types, which tend to be a bit thicker when cooked.

225 g/8 oz small, young okra

4 tsp ground coriander

1 large firm mango

3 tbsp olive oil

1 large onion, chopped

1 large red pepper, seeded, halved
   lengthwise and sliced

2 garlic cloves, crushed

2 green chilli peppers, seeded and
   chopped

4 tsp chopped fresh oregano

salt and freshly ground black pepper

1 lime, cut into wedges, to serve

≈ The okra must be small, firm, bright in colour and unblemished. Old fibrous or large okra will not cook successfully. Trim the stalk ends and points off the pods, then slice them thinly, and put in a bowl. Add the coriander, and toss well.

≈ The mango should be just ripe, but still firm (fruit that is soft or too sweet will not complement the okra). Peel the mango; then slice the flesh off the large, flat central pit. Cut the slices into small pieces.

≈ Heat the oil in a saucepan. Add the onion, pepper, garlic, chilli peppers and oregano; then cook, stirring occasionally for 10 minutes. Stir in the okra, and cook over a fairly high heat for about 3–5 minutes, until the okra slices are slightly browned in part, and just tender. Stir in the mango, taste for seasoning, and serve. Toss the okra mixture with the pasta; then arrange lime wedges around the edge of the dish so that their juice may be squeezed over to taste.

NUTRITION FACTS	
Amount per Serving	
Calories 135	Calories from Fat 80

	% Daily Value
Total Fat 9g	14%
Saturated Fat 1g	5%
Polyunsaturated Fat 1g	0%
Monounsaturated Fat 6g	0%
Cholesterol 0mg	0%
Sodium 17mg	0.7%
Total Carbohydrate 11g	4%
Dietary Fibre 1.5g	6%
Sugars 8g	0%
Protein 3g	0%

Percent daily values are based on a 2000 calorie diet

SPICY STUFFED TOMATOES

SERVES 4

Beefsteak tomatoes are perfect for stuffing and can be served as a vegetable main dish, accompaniment, or an appetizer. To make the tomatoes stand up in the dish, slice off the bottom of each one.

50 g/2 oz dried pastina (any tiny shapes)

dash of olive oil

4 large beefsteak tomatoes

Filling

2 medium potatoes, peeled and cut into cubes

4 tbsp olive oil

2 cloves of garlic, crushed

1 onion, finely chopped

2 tsp mild curry powder

pinch of ground cumin

1 tbsp tomato paste

4 tbsp chopped, fresh cilantro

salt and freshly ground black pepper

≈ Bring a saucepan of water to the boil, and add the pasta with a dash of olive oil. Cook for about 8 minutes, stirring occasionally, until tender. Drain and set aside.

≈ Slice the tops off the tomatoes and reserve. Using a teaspoon, scrape out the flesh of each tomato and reserve. Arrange the hollowed tomatoes in an oiled ovenproof dish, and set aside.

≈ To make the filling, cook the potatoes in boiling water for about 10 minutes, until tender. Drain and set aside. Heat the olive oil in a large frying pan, and sauté the garlic and onion for about 3 minutes, until softened.

≈ Add the curry powder, cumin and tomato paste. Cook for 2 minutes, then gently stir in the pasta and cooked potato. Add the chopped coriander and season with salt and freshly ground black pepper. Cook for a further 2–3 minutes, stirring occasionally, then remove from the heat.

≈ Preheat the oven to 200°C/400°F/Gas Mark 6. Stuff the tomatoes with the filling, placing any extra in the bottom of the dish. Place the tomato lids on top and bake for about 20 minutes, or until heated through.

NUTRITION FACTS	
Amount per Serving	
Calories 260	Calories from Fat 117
	% Daily Value
Total Fat 13g	20%
Saturated Fat 2g	10%
Polyunsaturated Fat 1.5g	0%
Monounsaturated Fat 9g	0%
Cholesterol 0mg	0%
Sodium 40mg	2%
Total Carbohydrate 32g	11%
Dietary Fibre 5g	20%
Sugars 7g	0%
Protein 5g	0%

Percent daily values are based on a 2000 calorie diet

SPANISH BAKED VEGETABLES

SERVES 4

A time-tested method of making salad from cooked vegetables, they are baked on the barbecue in summer and then dressed to serve cold. The method is popular in Catalonia, too, where the dish is called escalivada. *Here they are baked in the oven and make a good vegetarian main course.*

3 small aubergines

3 green peppers

4 medium onions, darkest skin removed

4 large tomatoes

10 spring onions, tips trimmed

150 ml/5 fl oz olive oil

3 garlic cloves, bruised

juice of 1 lemon

salt and freshly ground black pepper

3 tbsp chopped fresh parsley

≈ Preheat the oven to 200°C/400°F/ Gas Mark 6. Put the aubergine, peppers, onions, tomatoes and trimmed spring onions into 1–2 roasting pans with the oil and garlic cloves. A big pan will need about 125 ml/4 fl oz water added to prevent burning.

≈ Bake them for 25 minutes, then remove the tomatoes (you may also be able to combine ingredients from both pans at this point). After another 15 minutes, remove the peppers. Give the other vegetables a squeeze to see how close they are to being done. Put the peppers into a plastic bag; this will help with the skinning later.

≈ The aubergine will probably be ready in about another 15 minutes; the onions usually need another 15 minutes or more. Stir the juices in the roasting pan and pour them into a cup, discarding the garlic cloves.

≈ Skin the tomatoes, keeping them whole, and arrange them in the centre of a big platter, then just cut them across like a star. Skin the rest of the vegetables, slice them lengthwise, and keep all the juices they exude. Arrange the vegetables on the platter, radiating round the tomatoes. Arrange the aubergine so its seeds face upwards.

≈ Sprinkle lemon juice over the salad and season. Then stir the reserved juices, and dribble some onto the centre of the tomatoes and over the salad. Sprinkle with parsley and serve cold.

NUTRITION FACTS	
Amount per Serving	
Calories 445	Calories from Fat 360
	% Daily Value
Total Fat 40g	61%
Saturated Fat 6g	30%
Polyunsaturated Fat 4g	0%
Monounsaturated Fat 28g	0%
Cholesterol 0mg	0%
Sodium 22mg	1%
Total Carbohydrate 17g	6%
Dietary Fibre 11g	44%
Sugars 15g	0%
Protein 5g	0%

Percent daily values are based on a 2000 calorie diet

PASTA-STUFFED CABBAGE LEAVES

SERVES 4

Easy to prepare and sure to impress guests, this dish can be made a day in advance and kept in the refrigerator. Allow an extra 15–20 minutes to reheat in the oven before serving.

50 g/2 oz dried gnocchetti sardi
   (dumpling shapes) and/or pastina
   (any tiny shapes)
dash of olive oil
8 large savoy cabbage leaves, stalks
   removed

Filling

2 tbsp olive oil
2 cloves of garlic, crushed
2 carrots, peeled and grated
2 courgettes, grated
4 tomatoes, skinned, seeded, and
   chopped
50 g/2 oz chopped walnuts
salt and freshly ground black pepper

Sauce

400 g/14-oz can chopped tomatoes
4 tbsp dry red wine
150 ml/5 fl oz vegetable stock
1 tbsp dried oregano
1 onion, very finely chopped
salt and freshly ground black pepper

≈ Bring a large saucepan of water to the boil, and add the pasta with a dash of olive oil. Cook for about 10 minutes, stirring occasionally, until tender. Drain and set aside.

≈ Blanch the cabbage leaves in boiling water, then quickly immerse in cold water and drain. Pat dry with paper towels, and set aside.

≈ To make the filling, heat the olive oil in a large frying pan and sauté the garlic for about 1 minute. Add the grated carrots and courgettes, and cook for a further 3–4 minutes, stirring occasionally, until tender.

≈ Add the chopped tomatoes, walnuts and pasta. Season with salt and freshly ground black pepper. Cook for about 5 minutes, stirring occasionally, then set aside to cool.

≈ To make the sauce, place all the ingredients in a saucepan and bring to a simmer. Cook for 20–30 minutes, stirring occasionally, until reduced and thickened. Allow to cool slightly, then transfer to a food processor or blender and purée until smooth. Set aside.

≈ Preheat the oven to 200°C/400°F/Gas Mark 6.

≈ To assemble the stuffed cabbage leaves, lay the blanched leaves out on a work surface, concave side uppermost, and divide the mixture among the leaves, placing some of it in the centre of each leaf. Fold the edges of each leaf over to completely encase the filling.

≈ Arrange the stuffed leaves in a shallow ovenproof dish, and pour the sauce around the edges. Cover with foil and bake for about 20 minutes, until heated through. Serve immediately, with any extra sauce served separately.

NUTRITION FACTS	
Amount per Serving	
Calories 266	Calories from Fat 145

	% Daily Value
Total Fat 16g	25%
Saturated Fat 2g	10%
Polyunsaturated Fat 6.5g	0%
Monounsaturated Fat 6g	0%
Cholesterol 0mg	0%
Sodium 64mg	3%
Total Carbohydrate 23g	8%
Dietary Fibre 8g	32%
Sugars 13g	0%
Protein 7g	0%

Percent daily values are based on a 2000 calorie diet

AUBERGINE RAGOUT

SERVES 4

This richly flavoured dish should be accompanied at the table by plenty of fresh bread, feta cheese and a full-bodied red wine.

3 aubergines

salt

125 ml/4 fl oz olive oil

2 onions, halved and sliced

4 garlic cloves, crushed

675 g/1½ lb tomatoes, peeled, seeded, and chopped

3 tbsp chopped fresh parsley

salt and freshly ground black pepper, to taste

NUTRITION FACTS	
Amount per Serving	
Calories 302	Calories from Fat 250
	% Daily Value
Total Fat 28g	43%
Saturated Fat 4g	20%
Polyunsaturated Fat 3g	0%
Monounsaturated Fat 20g	0%
Cholesterol 0mg	0%
Sodium 18mg	0.75%
Total Carbohydrate 10g	3%
Dietary Fibre 6g	24%
Sugars 9g	0%
Protein 3g	0%

Percent daily values are based on a 2000 calorie diet

≈ Cut the aubergine into thick chunks and place in a colander. Generously sprinkle with salt and set aside for 30–45 minutes. Rinse the aubergine under cold running water and drain well.

≈ Heat the olive oil in a large saucepan and add the onion. Cook for 3–5 minutes, or until the onion has softened, then add the aubergine; stir to coat.

≈ Add the garlic, tomatoes and parsley to the saucepan and season with salt and freshly ground black pepper. Add a little water to moisten the mixture, if necessary, then cover and simmer for about 50–55 minutes, or until the aubergine is very soft and the sauce has thickened. Serve warm or cold.

BAKED MIXED VEGETABLES

SERVES 6

This light and easy-to-prepare dish is a favourite throughout Greece during spring and summer.

6 tbsp olive oil

3 onions, sliced

675 g/1½ lb small potatoes, peeled and halved, or cut into thick slices

675 g/1½ lb courgettes, cut into chunks

8 ripe tomatoes, peeled and roughly chopped

2 peppers, seeded and sliced into rings

4 garlic cloves, finely chopped

1 tsp dried oregano

4 tbsp chopped fresh parsley

2 tbsp chopped fresh dill

salt and freshly ground black pepper, to taste

125 ml/4 fl oz water

≈ Preheat the oven to 180°C/350°F/ Gas Mark 4. Heat 2 tbsp of the olive oil in a skillet and sauté the onion for 3–5 minutes, until softened but not coloured. Remove from the heat.

≈ Combine the sautéed onion with the prepared potatoes, courgettes, tomatoes, peppers, garlic, herbs and seasoning in a large roasting pan. Add the water and bake for 1½–2 hours, until the vegetables are tender and cooked through. Stir the vegetables around occasionally to cook through evenly. Serve warm or cold.

NUTRITION FACTS	
Amount per Serving	
Calories 239	Calories from Fat 108
	% Daily Value
Total Fat 12g	18%
Saturated Fat 2g	10%
Polyunsaturated Fat 2g	0%
Monounsaturated Fat 8g	0%
Cholesterol 0mg	0%
Sodium 27mg	1%
Total Carbohydrate 28g	9%
Dietary Fibre 7g	28%
Sugars 10g	0%
Protein 6g	0%

Percent daily values are based on a 2000 calorie diet

LAYERED AUBERGINE, POTATO AND TOMATO CASSEROLE

SERVES 6

In the Mediterranean aubergine dishes date from the time of the Moors. This one must have been updated when tomatoes, peppers and potatoes were introduced from America. It is typical of the solid soups and vegetable dishes of the islands, made in the earthenware greixonera.

2 aubergines

salt and freshly ground black pepper

9 small potatoes, peeled and sliced

2 large onions, chopped

100 ml/4 fl oz olive oil

2 garlic cloves, finely chopped

2 green peppers, seeded and sliced

1 red pepper, seeded and sliced

4 tbsp chopped parsley

3 400 g/14-oz cans tomatoes

2 tsp paprika

60 ml/2 fl oz red-wine vinegar

≈ Slice the aubergines very thinly, lay the slices out on a cutting board, and sprinkle with salt. Leave to sweat for 30–40 minutes, then blot with paper towels. Prepare the potatoes and cook them for 15 minutes in boiling salted water. Soften the onions in 2 tbsp oil over a low heat, then add the garlic.

≈ Grease an earthenware dish or casserole (30 cm/12 in across, by 7 cm/ 3 in deep) with oil. Make three layers of vegetables, starting with a third of the potato slices, then the aubergine slices, then the peppers, cooked onion and garlic, plus parsley. Add 1 can tomatoes and juice, squeezing the tomatoes through clenched fingers to break them up well. Season with salt, pepper and the paprika. Repeat until all ingredients are in. Sprinkle vinegar over the second layer and 1–1½ tbsps of oil over the top of the dish.

≈ Cover with foil and bake in a preheated oven at 200°C/400°F/ Gas Mark 6 for 1 hour. Then remove the foil, turn down the heat to 170°C/325°F/Gas Mark 3, and give it another 30–60 minutes, to brown and concentrate the juices. Excellent hot or cold, this dish also reheats well.

NUTRITION FACTS	
Amount per Serving	
Calories 267	Calories from Fat 170
	% Daily Value
Total Fat 19g	29%
Saturated Fat 3g	15%
Polyunsaturated Fat 2g	0%
Monounsaturated Fat 13g	0%
Cholesterol 0mg	0%
Sodium 90mg	3%
Total Carbohydrate 20.5g	7%
Dietary Fibre 6.5g	26%
Sugars 12g	0%
Protein 4.5g	0%

Percent daily values are based on a 2000 calorie diet

PROVENÇAL GREEN BEANS WITH PASTA

SERVES 4

A delicious way to serve green beans, piping hot with freshly grated Parmesan cheese.

3 tbsp olive oil

3 cloves of garlic, crushed

1 onion, chopped

3 tbsp chopped, fresh thyme

450 g/1 lb green beans

400 g/14-oz can chopped tomatoes

2 heaped tbsp tomato paste

450 ml/16 fl oz vegetable stock

150 ml/5 fl oz dry red wine

salt and freshly ground black pepper

450 g/1 lb dried pasta (any shapes)

freshly grated Parmesan cheese

≈ Heat 2 tbsp oil in a large pan and sauté the garlic and onion for about 3 minutes until softened. Add the thyme, beans, tomatoes, tomato paste, vegetable stock and wine, season with salt and freshly ground black pepper, and stir well to combine.

≈ Cover and cook gently for 25–30 minutes, until the beans are tender. Remove the lid and cook for a further 5–8 minutes, stirring occasionally, until the sauce has thickened slightly.

≈ Meanwhile, bring a large saucepan of water to the boil, and add the pasta with a dash of olive oil. Cook for about 10 minutes, stirring occasionally, until tender. Drain and return to the saucepan. Toss in oil and freshly ground black pepper.

≈ Serve the beans with the hot, buttered pasta and freshly grated Parmesan cheese.

NUTRITION FACTS	
Amount per Serving	
Calories 598	Calories from Fat 135
	% Daily Value
Total Fat 15g	23%
Saturated Fat 3g	15%
Polyunsaturated Fat 2g	0%
Monounsaturated Fat 9g	0%
Cholesterol 5mg	2%
Sodium 133mg	5.5%
Total Carbohydrate 95g	32%
Dietary Fibre 10g	40%
Sugars 10g	0%
Protein 20g	0%

Percent daily values are based on a 2000 calorie diet

FUSILLI WITH SUN-DRIED TOMATOES

SERVES 4

450 g/1 lb dried fusilli (pasta twists)

olive oil

2 tbsp tomato pesto

175 g/6-oz jar sun-dried tomatoes, drained and chopped

4 plum tomatoes, sliced into wedges

4 tbsp chopped, fresh basil

salt and freshly ground black pepper

A dish that is delicious served warm as a main course or cold as a summer salad.

≈ Bring a large saucepan of water to the boil and add the pasta with a dash of olive oil. Cook for about 10 minutes, stirring occasionally until tender. Drain and return to the saucepan.
≈ Stir in the remaining ingredients, drizzle with olive oil and serve warm immediately, or cool and refrigerate to serve chilled, if preferred.

NUTRITION FACTS	
Amount per Serving	
Calories 673	Calories from Fat 270
	% Daily Value
Total Fat 30g	46%
Saturated Fat 4.5g	22%
Polyunsaturated Fat 14g	0%
Monounsaturated Fat 9g	0%
Cholesterol 3mg	1%
Sodium 494mg	20%
Total Carbohydrate 90g	30%
Dietary Fibre 6g	24%
Sugars 6g	0%
Protein 17g	0%

Percent daily values are based on a 2000 calorie diet

KIDNEY BEAN, ARTICHOKE AND MUSHROOM CASSEROLE

SERVES 4

175 g/6 oz kidney beans

1–2 tbsp oil

1 large onion, chopped

1–2 cloves garlic, chopped

225 g/8 oz mushrooms, sliced

175 g/6 oz green beans, trimmed, cut in thirds and parboiled

425 g/15-oz can artichoke hearts

425 g/15-oz can tomatoes, mashed

salt and freshly ground black pepper

parsley

≈ Soak the kidney beans overnight and cook until tender.
≈ Preheat the oven to 180°C/350°F/ Gas Mark 4. Heat oil in a pan and fry onion and garlic until translucent. Add the mushrooms and stir-fry for 1–2 minutes until they begin to soften.
≈ Transfer all the ingredients to a casserole. Season well. Cover and bake for 30–40 minutes. Sprinkle with parsley and serve with baked potatoes and a green salad.

NUTRITION FACTS	
Amount per Serving	
Calories 279	Calories from Fat 45
	% Daily Value
Total Fat 5g	8%
Saturated Fat 1g	5%
Polyunsaturated Fat 3g	0%
Monounsaturated Fat 1g	0%
Cholesterol 0mg	0%
Sodium 56mg	2%
Total Carbohydrate 44g	15%
Dietary Fibre 21g	84%
Sugars 8g	0%
Protein 18g	0%

Percent daily values are based on a 2000 calorie diet

SPAGHETTI WITH TOMATOES

SERVES 4

This is a vegetarian version of a simple yet classic Italian dish.

350 g/¾ lb spaghetti (long tubes)

dash of olive oil

2 cloves of garlic, crushed

1 onion, finely chopped

450 g/1 lb carton sieved tomatoes

4 tbsp chopped, fresh basil

salt and freshly ground black pepper

80 g/3 oz freshly grated Parmesan
cheese

NUTRITION FACTS	
Amount per Serving	
Calories 511	Calories from Fat 140
	% Daily Value
Total Fat 15.5g	24%
Saturated Fat 8g	40%
Polyunsaturated Fat 1g	0%
Monounsaturated Fat 5g	0%
Cholesterol 38mg	13%
Sodium 430mg	18%
Total Carbohydrate 71g	24%
Dietary Fibre 6g	24%
Sugars 6g	0%
Protein 26g	0%

Percent daily values are based on a 2000 calorie diet

≈ Bring a large saucepan of water to the boil and add the pasta with a dash of olive oil. Cook for about 10 minutes, stirring occasionally until tender. Drain and set aside.

≈ Preheat the oven to 200°C/400°F/ Gas Mark 6. Place the garlic, onion, sieved tomatoes, basil and salt and freshly ground black pepper in a large pan, and heat until simmering. Cook for about 5 minutes, then remove from the heat.

≈ Arrange the pasta in a shallow, oiled, ovenproof dish. Curl it around to fit the dish, until the dish is tightly packed with the pasta.

≈ Spoon the tomato mixture over the top, pushing the pasta to ensure the sauce sinks down to the bottom of the dish. Sprinkle with the grated cheese, and bake for 25–30 minutes, until bubbling, crisp and golden. Cut in wedges, like a cake, to serve.

TAGLIATELLE NEAPOLITAN

SERVES 4

Yellow tomatoes make this dish look particularly attractive, although red ones taste just as good. If you can't find fresh tagliatelle, use the dried egg version.

450 g/1 lb fresh, multicoloured
   tagliatelle

dash of olive oil, plus 2 tbsp

2 cloves of garlic, crushed

1 onion, chopped

3 tbsp chopped, fresh basil or
   oregano

450 g/1 lb yellow and red tomatoes,
   skinned, seeded and chopped

225 g/8-oz carton chopped tomatoes

salt and freshly ground black pepper

fresh basil, to garnish

freshly grated Parmesan cheese, to
   serve

≈ Bring a large saucepan of water to the boil and add the tagliatelle with a dash of olive oil. Cook for about 5 minutes, stirring occasionally until tender. Drain and set aside, covered.

≈ Heat the remaining oil in a large pan, and sauté the garlic, onion and basil or oregano for about 3 minutes, or until the onion has softened.

≈ Add the chopped tomato flesh and drained tomatoes and season with salt and freshly ground black pepper. Stir and cook for about 10 minutes, until thickened and bubbling. Serve with the tagliatelle. Garnish with fresh basil and sprinkle with freshly grated Parmesan cheese.

NUTRITION FACTS	
Amount per Serving	
Calories 510	Calories from Fat 100
	% Daily Value
Total Fat 11g	17%
Saturated Fat 2g	10%
Polyunsaturated Fat 2g	0%
Monounsaturated Fat 6g	0%
Cholesterol 5mg	2%
Sodium 100mg	4%
Total Carbohydrate 92g	31%
Dietary Fibre 7g	28%
Sugars 8g	0%
Protein 17g	0%

Percent daily values are based on a 2000 calorie diet

PASTA PAELLA

SERVES 6

Based on the classic Spanish recipe, this dish makes a delicious, nutritious alternative, using pasta as the main ingredient. Any pasta shape will do; or use a combination of shapes for extra texture.

450 g/1 lb dried farfalle or bowtie pasta

1 tsp ground turmeric

dash of olive oil, plus 3 tbsp

2 cloves of garlic, crushed

1 onion

1 red pepper, seeded and chopped

100 g/4 oz baby carrots

16 baby corn

100 g/4 oz mange tout

100 g/4 oz fresh asparagus tips

50 g/2 oz pitted black olives

3 level tsp flour

≈ Bring a large saucepan of water to the boil, and add the pasta with the ground turmeric and a dash of olive oil. Cook for about 10 minutes, stirring occasionally, until tender. Drain, reserving the cooking liquid.

≈ Heat the remaining olive oil in a large pan and sauté the garlic and onion for about 3 minutes, until softened. Add the pepper, carrots and corn, and stir to combine. Cook for 2–3 minutes, then stir in the mange tout, asparagus tips, black olives and pasta. Cook for 2–3 minutes, then sprinkle with the flour and mix it into the vegetable mixture. Cook for 1 minute, then gradually stir in a little less than 450 ml/16 fl oz of the reserved pasta cooking liquid. Cook for 2–3 minutes, until the sauce is bubbling and thickened.

≈ Serve straight from the pan, or transfer to a warmed serving dish.

NUTRITION FACTS	
Amount per Serving	
Calories 396	Calories from Fat 135
	% Daily Value
Total Fat 9g	14%
Saturated Fat 1g	5%
Polyunsaturated Fat 1.5g	0%
Monounsaturated Fat 5g	0%
Cholesterol 0mg	0%
Sodium 395mg	16%
Total Carbohydrate 70.5g	23%
Dietary Fibre 7g	28%
Sugars 7g	0%
Protein 12g	0%

Percent daily values are based on a 2000 calorie diet

STUFFED SQUASH

SERVES 4

The word "squash" comes from the Native American "green thing eaten green". There are many varieties but for this recipe, choose a hard-skinned, winter squash. Do not peel the outer skin which forms a perfect case.

1 squash

salt and freshly ground black pepper

175 g/6 oz brown rice

2 small carrots, diced

25 g/1 oz peas

1–2 tbsp oil

1 onion, chopped

1 clove garlic, chopped

1 stick celery, chopped

1 handful parsley, chopped

2 tbsp hazelnuts, chopped

Tomato Sauce

1–2 tbsp oil

1 onion, chopped

2 cloves garlic, chopped

425 g/15-oz can tomatoes, mashed

1 tbsp tomato paste

salt and freshly ground black pepper

≈ Preheat the oven to 180°C/350°F/ Gas Mark 4. Cut the squash in half lengthwise and scoop out the pith and seeds. Sprinkle the flesh with salt and leave the halves upside down to drain.

≈ Meanwhile, make the filling. Simmer the rice in a covered pan of salted water until just tender (about 30 minutes). Drain.

≈ Parboil carrots and peas and drain. Heat oil in a pan and fry onion and garlic until translucent. Add celery, carrots and peas. Stir in the rice, parsley and hazelnuts and season well. Dry the squash and pile filling into one half of it. Top with second half.

≈ Make the tomato sauce. Heat oil in a pan and add onion and garlic. Fry, stirring, until soft. Add tomatoes and tomato paste. Simmer for 5 minutes stirring occasionally, and season well.

≈ Place squash in a baking dish with a lid, if you have one big enough, otherwise use foil to cover. Surround it with the sauce. Cover and cook for 45 minutes until tender. Serve hot or cold with a crisp green salad.

NUTRITION FACTS	
Amount per Serving	
Calories 265	Calories from Fat 135
	% Daily Value
Total Fat 15g	23%
Saturated Fat 2g	10%
Polyunsaturated Fat 8g	0%
Monounsaturated Fat 5g	0%
Cholesterol 0mg	0%
Sodium 60mg	2.5%
Total Carbohydrate 28g	9%
Dietary Fibre 6g	24%
Sugars 11g	0%
Protein 5g	0%

Percent daily values are based on a 2000 calorie diet

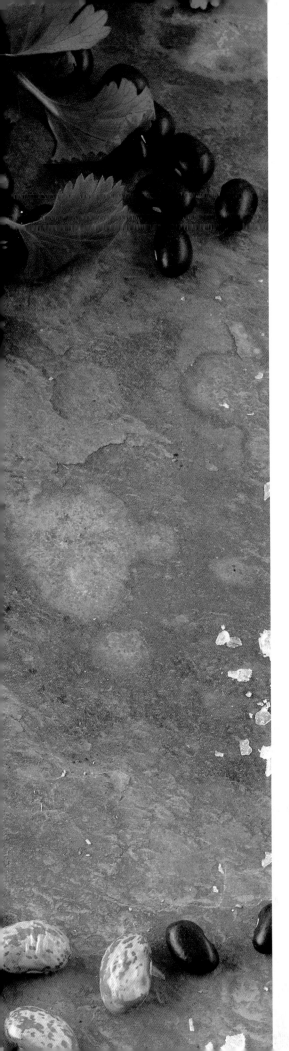

SIDE DISHES

Pasta with Broccoli and Tomatoes

Three Peppers in Tomato and Garlic

Spaghettini with Pine nuts

Pepper and Pasta Ratatouille

Artichokes with Tomato Sauce

Pasta with Pepper Sauce and Olives

Roast Potatoes in Sweet, Hot Sauce

Courgettes with Dill

Buckwheat Noodles with Savoy Cabbage

Spanish Green Beans

Tagliatelle with Lentil Sauce

Pasta with Green Peppers and Pesto

Tagliarini with Green Beans and Garlic

Greek Mushrooms

French Peas with Lettuce

Onions Roasted in Red Wine

Tangy Beans and Pasta

Patty Pan and Avocado Topping

Aubergine Stuffed with Garlic and Tomato

PASTA WITH BROCCOLI AND TOMATOES

SERVES 4

A lovely light lunch or supper dish. Choose vivid green, tightly packed heads of broccoli, and cook as briefly as possible to retain the colour and crisp texture.

350 g/¾ lb dried gnocchetti (dumpling shapes)

3 tbsp olive oil

350 g/¾ lb small broccoli florets

1 clove of garlic, chopped

2 tsp chopped, fresh rosemary

2 tsp chopped, fresh oregano

salt and freshly ground black pepper

200 g/7-oz can chopped tomatoes

1 tbsp tomato paste

fresh herbs, to garnish

NUTRITION FACTS	
Amount per Serving	
Calories 420	Calories from Fat 100
	% Daily Value
Total Fat 11g	17%
Saturated Fat 2g	10%
Polyunsaturated Fat 2g	0%
Monounsaturated Fat 6g	0%
Cholesterol 0mg	0%
Sodium 48mg	2%
Total Carbohydrate 70g	23%
Dietary Fibre 8g	32%
Sugars 5g	0%
Protein 15g	0%

Percent daily values are based on a 2000 calorie diet

≈ Bring a large saucepan of water to the boil and add the gnocchetti sardi with a dash of olive oil. Cook for about 6 minutes, stirring occasionally, until tender. Drain and return to the saucepan, covered, to keep warm.

≈ Meanwhile, heat the oil in a large pan. Add the broccoli, garlic, rosemary and oregano, and season with salt and pepper. Cover and cook gently for about 5 minutes, until tender.

≈ Add the chopped tomatoes and tomato paste, and stir. Add the pasta, mix together lightly, then serve immediately, garnished with fresh herbs.

THREE PEPPERS IN TOMATO AND GARLIC

SERVES 4

This is a summer tapa, a traditional Spanish dish, and may be eaten hot or cold; its flavour improves after one day. If you like spicy food, substitute chilli oil for the olive oil.

≈ Heat the oil in a large pan and cook the peppers gently for 2–3 minutes, stirring frequently. Add the parsley and garlic and cook for another couple of minutes.

≈ Add the chopped tomatoes and their juice to the pan. Stir and season.

≈ Cover the pan and simmer gently for about 20 minutes, until the peppers are tender.

≈ The sauce should be quite thick – if necessary, remove the peppers and boil rapidly to reduce the liquid. Check the seasoning.

50 ml/2 fl oz olive oil

2 yellow peppers, seeded and cut into thin strips

2 red peppers, seeded and cut into thin strips

2 green peppers, seeded and cut into thin strips

1 tbsp parsley, chopped

2 tsp garlic, crushed

225 g/8-oz (fresh or canned) tomatoes

salt and pepper

NUTRITION FACTS	
Amount per Serving	
Calories 450	Calories from Fat 324
	% Daily Value
Total Fat 36g	55%
Saturated Fat 5g	25%
Polyunsaturated Fat 4g	0%
Monounsaturated Fat 25g	0%
Cholesterol 0mg	0%
Sodium 44mg	2%
Total Carbohydrate 28g	9%
Dietary Fibre 13g	52%
Sugars 26g	0%
Protein 6g	0%

Percent daily values are based on a 2000 calorie diet

SPAGHETTINI WITH PINE NUTS

SERVES 4

450 g/1 lb dried multicoloured
 spaghettini

dash of olive oil

2 tbsp olive oil

1 clove of garlic, crushed

1 small onion, very finely chopped

75 g/3 oz pine nuts

225 g/8-oz can chopped tomatoes

salt and freshly ground black pepper

4 tbsp chopped, fresh basil

2 tbsp chopped, fresh parsley

Pine nuts give this dish its special taste and texture. Serve it straight from the pan.

NUTRITION FACTS	
Amount per Serving	
Calories 622	Calories from Fat 230
	% Daily Value
Total Fat 25.5g	39%
Saturated Fat 3g	15%
Polyunsaturated Fat 9g	0%
Monounsaturated Fat 12g	0%
Cholesterol 0mg	0%
Sodium 26mg	1%
Total Carbohydrate 87g	29%
Dietary Fibre 6g	24%
Sugars 7g	0%
Protein 17g	0%

Percent daily values are based on a 2000 calorie diet

≈ Bring a large saucepan of water to the boil and add the dried spaghettini with a dash of olive oil. Cook for about 10 minutes, stirring occasionally, until tender. Drain, and set aside.

≈ Heat the oil in a large pan and sauté the garlic and onion for about 3 minutes, or until the onion has softened. Add the pine nuts and stir-fry until evenly golden.

≈ Add the drained tomatoes, herbs and salt and freshly ground black pepper, and cook for about 5 minutes, stirring occasionally.

≈ Add the spaghettini and stir well to coat in the tomato sauce. Cook for a further 5 minutes, then serve immediately.

PEPPER AND PASTA RATATOUILLE

SERVES 4

Served with a hot, buttered baked potato, this simple dish is perfectly delicious.

150 g/1 lb dried wholewheat gnocchi piccoli (small shells)

dash of olive oil, plus 3 tbsp

2 cloves of garlic, crushed

1 onion, chopped

2 green peppers, seeded and cut into chunks

400 g/14-oz can chopped tomatoes

2 tbsp tomato paste

150 ml/5 fl oz dry red wine

2 tbsp fresh oregano

salt and freshly ground black pepper

fresh oregano sprigs, to garnish

≈ Bring a large saucepan of water to the boil and add the pasta with a dash of olive oil. Cook for about 10 minutes, stirring occasionally, until tender. Drain and set aside.

≈ Heat the remaining olive oil in a large saucepan and sauté the garlic and onion for about 3 minutes, until softened. Stir in the pepper chunks. Cover and cook for about 5 minutes.

≈ Stir the remaining ingredients, except the oregano sprigs, into the pepper mixture and bring to simmering point. Reduce the heat, cover and cook for about 10 minutes, then stir in the pasta. Cook for a further 5 minutes, stirring occasionally. Serve garnished with fresh oregano sprigs.

NUTRITION FACTS	
Amount per Serving	
Calories 544	Calories from Fat 108
	% Daily Value
Total Fat 12g	18%
Saturated Fat 2g	10%
Polyunsaturated Fat 2g	0%
Monounsaturated Fat /g	0%
Cholesterol 0mg	0%
Sodium 70mg	3%
Total Carbohydrate 93g	31%
Dietary Fibre 8g	32%
Sugars 9g	0%
Protein 16g	0%

Percent daily values are based on a 2000 calorie diet

ARTICHOKES WITH TOMATO SAUCE

SERVES 4

4 large artichokes

1–2 tbsp oil

1 large onion, chopped

2 cloves garlic, chopped

425 g/15-oz can tomatoes

1 tbsp tomato paste

2 tsp fresh oregano, chopped

lemon juice

salt and freshly ground black pepper

≈ Rinse the artichokes thoroughly under cold water and leave them upside down to drain. Bring a very large pan of salted water to the boil, put the artichokes in and boil vigorously for 30–50 minutes, depending on the size. When an outer leaf comes away at a gentle tug, the artichokes are ready.

≈ Meanwhile, make the sauce. Heat the oil in a pan and fry the onion and garlic until transparent. Add the tomatoes, tomato paste and oregano and reduce until the sauce is of pouring consistency but not sloppy. Season with salt and pepper and a dash of lemon juice to taste.

~ Drain the artichokes. When cool, pull out the tiny inner leaves together with the hairy inedible choke. Spoon in some tomato sauce. Stand each artichoke in a pool of sauce on an individual dish and serve.

NUTRITION FACTS

Amount per Serving

Calories 92	Calories from Fat 45

	% Daily Value
Total Fat 5g	8%
Saturated Fat 1g	5%
Polyunsaturated Fat 0.5g	0%
Monounsaturated Fat 3g	0%
Cholesterol 0mg	0%
Sodium 54mg	2%
Total Carbohydrate 12g	4%
Dietary Fibre 4.5g	18%
Sugars 6g	0%
Protein 3g	0%

Percent daily values are based on a 2000 calorie diet

PASTA WITH PEPPER SAUCE AND OLIVES

SERVES 4

This low-fat Pepper Sauce helps to keep the calories in this dish down.

350 g/12 oz dried rigatoni (short tubes)

dash of olive oil

50 g/2 oz pitted black olives, chopped

grated cheese, to serve

Pepper Sauce

2 red peppers

4 cloves of garlic, peeled

300 ml/10 fl oz vegetable stock

salt and freshly ground black pepper

≈ Bring a large saucepan of water to the boil and add the rigatoni with a dash of olive oil. Cook for about 10 minutes, stirring occasionally, until tender. Drain and return to the saucepan. Set aside.

≈ Skin, de-seed and chop the peppers.

≈ To make the sauce, place the chopped pepper, garlic and vegetable stock in a food processor or blender, and season with salt and freshly ground black pepper. Purée until smooth.

≈ Stir the Pepper Sauce into the rigatoni with the chopped olives. Serve with grated cheese.

NUTRITION FACTS

Amount per Serving

Calories 487	Calories from Fat 72

	% Daily Value
Total Fat 8g	12%
Saturated Fat 3g	15%
Polyunsaturated Fat 1.5g	0%
Monounsaturated Fat 3g	0%
Cholesterol 10mg	3%
Sodium 336mg	14%
Total Carbohydrate 92g	31%
Dietary Fibre 7g	28%
Sugars 8g	0%
Protein 17g	0%

Percent daily values are based on a 2000 calorie diet

ROAST POTATOES IN SWEET HOT SAUCE

SERVES 4

riginating as Spanish peasant fare, called Patatas Bravas, *it is easy to see why this simple dish is so popular.*

1 onion, chopped

2 tbsp olive oil

1 bay leaf

2 red chilli peppers

2 tsp garlic

1 tbsp tomato paste

½ tbsp sugar (up to 1 tbsp, if the
    sauce is too tart for your liking)

1 tbsp soy sauce

425 g/15-oz can plum tomatoes,
    chopped

1 glass of white wine

salt and black pepper

8 medium potatoes

NUTRITION FACTS	
Amount per Serving	
Calories 254	Calories from Fat 54
	% Daily Value
Total Fat 6g	9%
Saturated Fat 1g	5%
Polyunsaturated Fat 1g	0%
Monounsaturated Fat 4g	0%
Cholesterol 0mg	0%
Sodium 70mg	3%
Total Carbohydrate 41g	14%
Dietary Fibre 5g	20%
Sugars 7g	0%
Protein 6g	0%

Percent daily values are based on a 2000 calorie diet

≈ To prepare the sauce, sweat the onions in the oil with the bay leaf. When soft, add the chilli peppers, garlic, tomato paste, sugar and soy sauce. Sweat for a further 5 minutes on a low heat.

≈ Add the chopped tomatoes and white wine. Stir and bring to the boil. Simmer for 10 minutes. Taste and season.

≈ This sauce should be slightly sweet; the flavour of the tomatoes should not dominate it.

≈ Cut the potatoes into chunks.

≈ Grease a baking tray. Season the potatoes well and brush with oil.

≈ Roast in a hot oven, 230°C/450°F/Gas Mark 8, until golden.

≈ Pour the tomato sauce over the potatoes and serve.

COURGETTES WITH DILL

Serves 4

This delicious vegetable dish could not be simpler to make. It's an ideal accompaniment to any main dish.

50 ml/2 fl oz olive oil

1 onion, chopped

1 tsp crushed garlic

450 g/1 lb courgettes, topped, tailed, and sliced in thickish rounds

½ tsp black pepper

2 tsp paprika

1 tbsp dill, chopped (not the stalks)

150 ml/5 fl oz soured cream

salt to taste

≈ Heat oil in a large pan. Cook the onion and garlic gently until soft. Turn up the heat.

≈ Add the courgettes, garlic and black pepper and toss.

≈ Cook for 5–10 minutes, stirring to cook both sides of the courgette slices.

≈ When brown, add the paprika, dill, and soured cream. Season and serve.

NUTRITION FACTS	
Amount per Serving	
Calories 228	Calories from Fat 200
	% Daily Value
Total Fat 22g	34%
Saturated Fat 7g	35%
Polyunsaturated Fat 2g	0%
Monounsaturated Fat 12g	0%
Cholesterol 23mg	8%
Sodium 17mg	0.7%
Total Carbohydrate 5g	2%
Dietary Fibre 2g	8%
Sugars 4g	0%
Protein 3g	0%

Percent daily values are based on a 2000 calorie diet

BUCKWHEAT NOODLES WITH SAVOY CABBAGE

SERVES 6

350 g/¾ lb buckwheat noodles

225 g/½ lb savoy cabbage, shredded

1 medium potato, peeled and diced

3 tbsp olive oil

4 tbsp chopped, fresh sage

pinch of freshly grated nutmeg

225 g/½ lb diced Fontina cheese

100 g/4 oz freshly grated Parmesan cheese

Buckwheat noodles, known as pizzoccheri, *are a speciality of northern Italy, and are available from Italian delicatessens. Wholewheat or egg tagliatelle make good substitutes.*

≈ Bring a large saucepan of water to the boil and add the buckwheat noodles, cabbage and potato with a dash of olive oil. Cook for 10–15 minutes, stirring occasionally, until tender. Drain and set aside, covered, to keep warm.

≈ Meanwhile, heat the oil in a large pan, and sauté the garlic and sage for about 1 minute. Remove from the heat and set aside.

≈ Place a layer of the pasta and vegetables in a warm serving dish and sprinkle with a little nutmeg, some of the Fontina cheese and some of the Parmesan cheese.

≈ Repeat the layers, then pour the hot garlic oil over the pasta. Mix lightly into the pasta and serve immediately.

NUTRITION FACTS	
Amount per Serving	
Calories 596	Calories from Fat 234
	% Daily Value
Total Fat 26g	40%
Saturated Fat 11g	55%
Polyunsaturated Fat 2g	0%
Monounsaturated Fat 8g	0%
Cholesterol 48mg	16%
Sodium 774mg	32%
Total Carbohydrate 65g	22%
Dietary Fibre 19g	76%
Sugars 16g	0%
Protein 30g	0%

Percent daily values are based on a 2000 calorie diet

SPANISH GREEN BEANS

SERVES 4

450 g/1 lb green beans, topped and
  tailed

50 ml/2 fl oz olive oil

½ medium onion, finely sliced

salt and pepper to taste

300 ml/10 fl oz vegetable stock

1 tbsp garlic, crushed

≈ Place the beans in a pot of boiling salted water and cook for 6–8 minutes, until the beans are fairly firm but not raw. Drain well.

≈ Heat the oil in a pan. Add the onion, cook gently for 3–4 minutes. Add the beans, salt and pepper, and toss. Add the vegetable stock and the garlic.

≈ Cover and cook until tender, for about 10 minutes. Season well and serve.

NUTRITION FACTS	
Amount per Serving	
Calories 220	Calories from Fat 190
	% Daily Value
Total Fat 21g	32%
Saturated Fat 3g	15%
Polyunsaturated Fat 2g	0%
Monounsaturated Fat 15g	0%
Cholesterol 0mg	0%
Sodium 0mg	0%
Total Carbohydrate 5g	2%
Dietary Fibre 4g	16%
Sugars 3g	0%
Protein 2.5g	0%

Percent daily values are based on a 2000 calorie diet

TAGLIATELLE WITH LENTIL SAUCE

SERVES 4

Here's a handy recipe you can rustle up in minutes.

350 g/¾ lb dried tagliatelle

dash of olive oil

Sauce

2 tbsp olive oil

2 cloves of garlic, crushed

1 large onion, very finely chopped

175 g/6 oz red lentils, washed and
    drained

3 tbsp tomato paste

salt and freshly ground black pepper

600 ml/1 pt boiling water

sprigs of fresh rosemary, to garnish

freshly grated Parmesan cheese, to
    serve

≈ Bring a large saucepan of water to the boil and add the tagliatelle with a dash of olive oil. Cook for about 10 minutes, stirring occasionally, until tender. Drain, and return to the saucepan. Set aside.

≈ To make the lentil sauce, heat the olive oil in a large saucepan and sauté the garlic and onion for about 5 minutes, stirring occasionally, until softened. Add the lentils, tomato paste, salt and freshly ground black pepper, and stir in the boiling water. Bring to the boil, then simmer for about 20 minutes, stirring occasionally, until the lentils have softened.

≈ Reheat the tagliatelle gently for 2–3 minutes, if necessary, then serve with the lentil sauce. Scatter a few sprigs of fresh rosemary over the top, and serve with freshly grated Parmesan cheese.

NUTRITION FACTS	
Amount per Serving	
Calories 553	Calories from Fat 100
	% Daily Value
Total Fat 11g	17%
Saturated Fat 2g	10%
Polyunsaturated Fat 2g	0%
Monounsaturated Fat 6g	0%
Cholesterol 5mg	2%
Sodium 117mg	5%
Total Carbohydrate 96g	32%
Dietary Fibre 8g	32%
Sugars 6.5g	0%
Protein 24g	0%

Percent daily values are based on a 2000 calorie diet

PASTA WITH GREEN PEPPERS AND PESTO

SERVES 4

If linguine is unavailable, spaghettini or tagliatelle will work just as well in this dish.

450 g/1 lb fresh linguine (thin, flat pasta strips)

dash of olive oil, plus 2 tbsp

2 cloves of garlic, crushed

2 tbsp pesto sauce

50 ml/2 fl oz vegetable stock

1 green pepper, deseeded and very thinly sliced

fresh herbs, to garnish

NUTRITION FACTS

Amount per Serving

Calories 494	Calories from Fat 108

	% Daily Value
Total Fat 12g	18%
Saturated Fat 2g	10%
Polyunsaturated Fat 2g	0%
Monounsaturated Fat 6.5g	0%
Cholesterol 3mg	1%
Sodium 45mg	2%
Total Carbohydrate 87g	29%
Dietary Fibre 6g	24%
Sugars 4g	0%
Protein 15g	0%

Percent daily values are based on a 2000 calorie diet

≈ Bring a large saucepan of water to the boil and add the linguine with a dash of olive oil. Cook for about 4 minutes, stirring occasionally, until tender. Drain and return to the saucepan. Stir in a dash more olive oil and set aside, covered, to keep warm.

≈ Heat the remaining olive oil in a large pan and sauté the garlic for 1–2 minutes, then stir in the pesto sauce. Add the vegetable stock, stir, and cook for 1 minute, then add the pepper slices. Cook for a further 7–10 minutes, stirring occasionally, until the pepper has softened. Stir the pepper mixture into the linguine and serve, garnished with fresh herbs.

TAGLIARINI WITH GREEN BEANS AND GARLIC

SERVES 4

A delicious summer salad, hot main course or vegetable accompaniment, this dish is suitable for almost any occasion.

350 g/¾ lb dried tagliarini (flat spaghetti)

dash of olive oil, plus 4 tbsp

350 g/¾ lb green beans

1 medium potato, cut into small cubes

3 cloves of garlic, chopped

5 tbsp chopped, fresh sage

salt and freshly ground black pepper

freshly grated Parmesan cheese, to serve

≈ Bring a large saucepan of water to the boil and add the tagliarini with a dash of olive oil. Cook for 10 minutes, stirring occasionally, until tender. Drain and set aside.

≈ Cook the beans and potato cubes in a large saucepan of boiling water for about 10 minutes, until tender. Drain well, and set aside to keep warm.

≈ Heat the remaining olive oil in a large pan, add the garlic and sage, and season with salt and freshly ground black pepper. Sauté for 2–3 minutes, then add the cooked beans and potato. Cook for 1–2 minutes, then add the cooked tagliarini and mix well.

≈ Cook for about 5 minutes, stirring occasionally, then transfer to a warmed serving dish. Sprinkle with freshly grated Parmesan cheese and serve.

NUTRITION FACTS	
Amount per Serving	
Calories 489	Calories from Fat 144
	% Daily Value
Total Fat 16g	25%
Saturated Fat 3g	15%
Polyunsaturated Fat 2g	0%
Monounsaturated Fat 10g	0%
Cholesterol 5mg	2%
Sodium 60mg	2.5%
Total Carbohydrate 76g	25%
Dietary Fibre 7g	28%
Sugars 5g	0%
Protein 15g	0%

Percent daily values are based on a 2000 calorie diet

GREEK MUSHROOMS

SERVES 6

Meze is a type of appetizer, eaten especially with an aperitif or other drink in Greece. It is best kept simple, with the use of fresh, firm mushrooms and a good-quality olive oil for the best flavour.

150 ml/5 fl oz olive oil

125 ml/4 fl oz dry white wine

salt and freshly ground black pepper, to taste

1 tsp dried thyme

3 garlic cloves, crushed

4 tbsp chopped fresh parsley

600 g/1¼ lb tiny button mushrooms, cleaned

freshly squeezed juice of 1 lemon

chopped fresh parsley, to garnish

NUTRITION FACTS	
Amount per Serving	
Calories 245	Calories from Fat 225
	% Daily Value
Total Fat 25g	38%
Saturated Fat 4g	20%
Polyunsaturated Fat 2g	0%
Monounsaturated Fat 18g	0%
Cholesterol 0mg	0%
Sodium 7mg	0.3%
Total Carbohydrate 1g	0.3%
Dietary Fibre 2g	8%
Sugars 0g	0%
Protein 2g	0%

Percent daily values are based on a 2000 calorie diet

≈ Place all the ingredients, except the mushrooms and half the lemon juice in a large saucepan and bring to the boil. Reduce the heat and stir in the mushrooms. Cover and simmer for 8–10 minutes.

≈ Transfer the mushrooms and the liquid to a serving dish and allow to cool completely. Serve at room temperature, sprinkled with the remaining lemon juice and garnished with chopped fresh parsley.

FRENCH PEAS WITH LETTUCE

SERVES 4

Thanks, no doubt, to the mass availability of the frozen variety, peas have become an all-too-familiar vegetable in some households. This version of the French way of cooking them gives them a culinary fillip.

≈ Blanch the peas and onions or shallots in boiling, salted water for 5 minutes, then drain.

≈ Put the peas, onions, lettuce, stock, and yogurt in a pan and season with salt and pepper. Bring to a boil, cover the pan and simmer gently for 10 minutes.

· Stir in the sugar and adjust the seasoning if necessary.

≈ Sprinkle with mint before serving.

1 kg/2¼ lb fresh peas, shelled

225 g/½ lb small onions or shallots, peeled and left whole

salt

8 outer lettuce leaves, torn into small pieces

6 tbsp vegetable stock

3 tbsp natural low-fat yogurt

black pepper

1 tsp sugar

Garnish

2 tbsp chopped mint

NUTRITION FACTS	
Amount per Serving	
Calories 246	Calories from Fat 36
	% Daily Value
Total Fat 4g	6%
Saturated Fat 1g	5%
Polyunsaturated Fat 2g	0%
Monounsaturated Fat 0.5g	0%
Cholesterol 1mg	0.3%
Sodium 20mg	0.8%
Total Carbohydrate 36g	12%
Dietary Fibre 18g	72%
Sugars 12g	0%
Protein 19g	0%

Percent daily values are based on a 2000 calorie diet

4 large Spanish onions

2 tbsp sunflower oil

180 ml/6 fl oz red wine

300 ml/10 fl oz vegetable stock

salt and black pepper

Garnish

parsley sprigs

NUTRITION FACTS	
Amount per Serving	
Calories 120	Calories from Fat 54
	% Daily Value
Total Fat 6g	9%
Saturated Fat 1g	5%
Polyunsaturated Fat 4g	0%
Monounsaturated Fat 1g	0%
Cholesterol 0mg	0%
Sodium 6mg	0.25%
Total Carbohydrate 10g	3%
Dietary Fibre 2g	8%
Sugars 7g	0%
Protein 1.5g	0%

Percent daily values are based on a 2000 calorie diet

ONIONS ROASTED IN RED WINE

SERVES 4

Oven roasted onions are an excellent complement to many main dishes.

≈ Preheat the oven to 170°C/325°F/Gas Mark 3. Peel the onions, and cut a thin slice from each base, so that they will stand upright.

≈ Heat the oil in a pan, and fry the onions on all sides over medium heat. Pour on the wine, bring to the boil and simmer for 2–3 minutes. Pour on the stock, season with salt and pepper, and bring back to the boil.

≈ If you have used a pan, transfer the onions and sauce to an ovenproof dish. Bake uncovered in the oven for 1¼–1½ hours until the onions are soft and the sauce has reduced and thickened. Serve hot, garnished with the parsley.

---

50 g/2 oz dried pastina (tiny shapes)

dash of olive oil

400 g/14-oz can mixed beans

1 red pepper

2 tsp dried oregano

Dressing

2 cloves of garlic, crushed

4 tbsp extra virgin olive oil

2–3 tbsp balsamic vinegar

1 tsp tomato paste

salt and freshly ground black pepper

NUTRITION FACTS	
Amount per Serving	
Calories 273	Calories from Fat 117
	% Daily Value
Total Fat 13g	20%
Saturated Fat 2g	10%
Polyunsaturated Fat 1.5g	0%
Monounsaturated Fat 9g	0%
Cholesterol 0mg	0%
Sodium 409mg	17%
Total Carbohydrate 30g	10%
Dietary Fibre 9g	36%
Sugars 6.5g	0%
Protein 10g	0%

Percent daily values are based on a 2000 calorie diet

TANGY BEANS AND PASTA

SERVES 4

Use tiny pasta shapes for this delicious and nutritious dish and serve with warm, crusty French bread.

≈ Bring a large saucepan of water to the boil and add the pastina with a dash of olive oil. Cook for about 8 minutes, stirring occasionally, until tender. Drain, and rinse under cold running water. Drain again, and place in a large mixing bowl.

≈ Deseed and chop the pepper. Add the beans, pepper and oregano to the pasta.

≈ Place all the dressing ingredients in a screw-top jar, and shake well to combine. Pour the dressing over the mixture, toss, and chill for at least 30 minutes before serving.

PATTY PAN AND AVOCADO TOPPING

SERVES 4

Small, yellow patty pan squash are complemented by the avocado in this sautéed mixture, which makes a colourful first course, or a light lunch or side dish. Halve the quantities if the mixture is served as a topping for a first-course portion of pasta. Fresh pasta shapes are the best base for this topping.

3 tbsp olive oil

2 onions, sliced

1 carrot, halved and thinly sliced

1 sprig of tarragon

450 g/1 lb patty pan squash, halved
    horizontally

salt and freshly ground black pepper

4 avocados

juice of ½ lemon

8 large sprigs of dill, chopped

NUTRITION FACTS	
Amount per Serving	
Calories 409	Calories from Fat 333
	% Daily Value
Total Fat 37g	57%
Saturated Fat 7g	35%
Polyunsaturated Fat 4g	0%
Monounsaturated Fat 24g	0%
Cholesterol 0mg	0%
Sodium 20mg	0.8%
Total Carbohydrate 16g	5%
Dietary Fibre 11g	44%
Sugars 9g	0%
Protein 4.5g	0%

Percent daily values are based on a 2000 calorie diet

≈ Heat the oil in a large saucepan. Add the onions, carrot and tarragon. Stir well, cover and cook for about 15 minutes, or until the onions have softened.

≈ Stir in the squash, salt and pepper to taste, and cover the pan; then continue to cook for a further 15 minutes, stirring once or twice, until the squash are tender but not too soft.

≈ Halve the avocados, remove their stones, and cut them into quarters lengthwise. Peel each segment of avocado and slice it crosswise. Sprinkle with the lemon juice. Stir the avocado into the squash mixture, add the dill and mix well. Then taste for seasoning before serving. Toss the vegetables into a large bowl of pasta, or spoon them on top of individual dishes of pasta.

AUBERGINE STUFFED WITH GARLIC AND TOMATO

SERVES 6

1 kg/2¼ lb aubergines
150 ml/5 fl oz olive oil
1 kg/2¼ lb tomatoes
4 cloves of garlic
2 tbsp chopped parsley
salt and black pepper to taste

≈ Preheat the oven to 200°C/400°F/ Gas Mark 6. Slice the aubergines in half lengthwise.

≈ Fry the aubergines in the oil – about 2 minutes per side at a high heat. Lift out the aubergine, drain, and allow to cool slightly.

≈ Remove the seeds from the tomatoes, dice and fry in the oil.

≈ Scoop out the aubergine flesh, leaving a shell ½ cm/¼ in thick. Reserve the shells.

≈ Crush the garlic and add, with the chopped flesh of the aubergines, to the tomatoes. Stir in the chopped parsley and season to taste with salt and freshly ground black pepper.

≈ Cook over a medium heat for about 5 minutes. Then scoop out the mixture with a slotted spoon, pressing out any excess oil, and fill each of the aubergine halves with some of it. Bake until the cases and filling are hot all the way through.

NUTRITION FACTS	
Amount per Serving	
Calories 260	Calories from Fat 216
	% Daily Value
Total Fat 24g	37%
Saturated Fat 4g	20%
Polyunsaturated Fat 2.5g	0%
Monounsaturated Fat 17g	0%
Cholesterol 0mg	0%
Sodium 19mg	0.8%
Total Carbohydrate 9g	3%
Dietary Fibre 7g	28%
Sugars 9g	0%
Protein 3g	0%

Percent daily values are based on a 2000 calorie diet

Desserts

Nut, Honey and Cinnamon Baklava Pastries

Fruit Parcels

Winter Fruit Compote with Tiny Pasta Shapes

Kumquats in Caramel

Honey and Orange Figs

Watermelon Granité

Tangerine and Ginger Sorbet

Fettuccine with Apple and Cinnamon Sauce

Continental Plum Cake

Citrus Jelly

Portuguese Peaches in Red Wine

Baked Stuffed Peaches

Tomato, Orange and Basil Sorbet

Golden Summer Pudding

Fresh Fruit Dessert Cake

Grape Custards

Lychee and Lime Sorbet

Melon, Kiwi Fruit and Grape Salad

Marzipan Candies

Honey, Orange and Almond Tagliatelle

Almond Petits Fours

NUT, HONEY AND CINNAMON BAKLAVA PASTRIES

MAKES ABOUT 24

A mixture of walnuts and almonds is used in this version of the classic Greek pastry but if you prefer you can stick to one or the other – or indeed, try using pistachios instead.

100 g/4 oz polyunsaturated
    margarine
450 g/1 lb filo pastry, thawed if
    frozen

Filling

4 tbsp clear honey
2 tbsp freshly squeezed lemon juice
50 g/2 oz caster sugar
2 tsp ground cinnamon
1 tsp finely grated lemon zest
100 g/4 oz blanched almonds,
    roughly chopped
100 g/4 oz shelled walnuts, roughly
    chopped

Syrup

400 g/14 oz caster sugar
5 tbsp clear honey
600 ml/1 pt water
1 cinnamon stick
strip of lemon peel

≈ Preheat the oven to 170°C/325°F/ Gas Mark 3. Grease a roasting pan. Trim the sheet of filo pastry dough to fit inside the pan and discard the trimmings.

≈ Place the first sheet of filo dough in the base of the prepared pan and brush evenly with melted margarine. Lay another sheet of filo on top and brush again with the melted margarine. Repeat this process until you have 12 sheets of filo pastry dough layered on the bottom of the pan. Cover the remaining filo pastry dough with a slightly damp cloth to prevent it from drying out while you work.

≈ To make the filling, place the honey in a medium-sized bowl. Add the lemon juice and stir until combined. Stir in the sugar, ground cinnamon, lemon zest and nuts. Spread half of the filling mixture over the filo in the base of the pan.

≈ Layer another three sheets of filo pastry dough on top of the filling, brushing each sheet with melted margarine. Spread the remaining filling mixture over the filo and cover with the remaining sheets of filo, brushing each sheet with melted margarine. Brush the top with any remaining margarine and score into 5 cm/2-inch diamond shapes. Bake for about 1 hour, or until crisp and golden. Remove from the oven and stand on a wire rack.

≈ To make the syrup, place all the ingredients together in a medium-sized saucepan and heat gently until the sugar has dissolved completely. Increase the heat and boil rapidly for about 10 minutes, without stirring. Set aside to cool. Discard the cinnamon stick and lemon peel and pour the syrup evenly over the pastry.

NUTRITION FACTS

Amount per Serving (each)

Calories 185	Calories from Fat 100

	% Daily Value
Total Fat 11g	17%
Saturated Fat 1.5g	7.5%
Polyunsaturated Fat 5g	0%
Monounsaturated Fat 4g	0%
Cholesterol 0mg	0%
Sodium 40mg	2%
Total Carbohydrate 20g	7%
Dietary Fibre 1g	4%
Sugars 8g	0%
Protein 4g	0%

Percent daily values are based on a 2000 calorie diet

FRUIT PARCELS

MAKES ABOUT 32

Dough

175 g/6 oz plain flour

pinch of salt

1 egg, beaten

3 tbsp water

Filling

225 g/8 oz fresh fruit, such as
cherries, plums, apricots, or
blueberries

icing sugar

soured cream, to serve

NUTRITION FACTS	
Amount per Serving	
Calories 21	Calories from Fat 3
	% Daily Value
Total Fat 0.3g	0.5%
Saturated Fat 0g	0%
Polyunsaturated Fat 0g	0%
Monounsaturated Fat 0g	0%
Cholesterol 7mg	2%
Sodium 3mg	0.1%
Total Carbohydrate 4g	1%
Dietary Fibre 0.5g	2%
Sugars 1g	0%
Protein 1g	0%

Percent daily values are based on a 2000 calorie diet

≈ Put the flour into a bowl, and mix in the salt. Make a well in the middle; then add the egg and water. Mix in the flour to form a dough; then knead well until smooth.

≈ Prepare the fruit according to type: stone cherries, halve and stone plums and apricots, rinse and dry blueberries.

≈ Roll out the dough into a circle on a lightly floured counter until it is roughly 40 cm/16-in across. Then stamp out 6 cm/2½-in rounds. Place a piece of fruit on each round, and brush the edges of the dough lightly with water. Then fold the dough around the fruit, and pinch the edges to seal them well.

≈ Cook the fruit parcels in boiling water for about 3 minutes, then drain well, and coat lightly with icing sugar; serve with soured cream as an accompaniment.

WINTER FRUIT COMPOTE WITH TINY PASTA SHAPES

SERVES 4

Try this for breakfast. It needs to be started the day before, and will keep for several days in the refrigerator. Make up your own selection of mixed dried fruit, if you prefer.

about 15 dried apricots

175 g/6 oz dried apple rings or
  chunks

about 12 dried pears

8 dried figs

50 g/2 oz dried cherries

4 cloves

2 allspice berries

1 cinnamon stick

finely grated zest and juice of
  1 orange

300 ml/10 fl oz weak tea

425 ml/15 fl oz water

3 tbsp soft brown sugar

4 tbsp dried pastina (any tiny shapes)

≈ Place the dried fruit in a bowl with the spices, orange zest and juice, tea and water. Cover and leave to soak overnight.

≈ The next day, spoon the compote into a saucepan, bring to the boil and simmer for 15 minutes, adding a little more water if necessary. Stir in the brown sugar and pastina, and cook for a further 8–10 minutes, until the pastina is tender. Serve warm or cold.

NUTRITION FACTS	
Amount per Serving	
Calories 432	Calories from Fat 13
	% Daily Value
Total Fat 1.5g	2%
Saturated Fat 0.5g	2.5%
Polyunsaturated Fat 0.5g	0%
Monounsaturated Fat 0.5g	0%
Cholesterol 0mg	0%
Sodium 61mg	2.5%
Total Carbohydrate 106g	35%
Dietary Fibre 18g	72%
Sugars 97g	0%
Protein 6g	0%

Percent daily values are based on a 2000 calorie diet

KUMQUATS IN CARAMEL

SERVES 4

Smallest of all the citrus fruits, kumquats are a good source of vitamins A and C, potassium, magnesium and calcium. Sliced and arranged in rings they make an unusual garnish. Their characteristic tartness is offset in this recipe by a delicious golden caramel sauce.

450 g/1 lb kumquats, washed and cut into thin slices
225 g/8 oz sugar
150 ml/5 fl oz cold water
150 ml/5 fl oz warm water
25 g/1 oz seedless raisins

Decoration
bay leaf

≈ Put the sugar and cold water into a medium-sized, heavy-based pan. Dissolve the sugar slowly over low heat, stirring occasionally. Bring to the boil and boil steadily until caramel coloured (about 5 minutes).

≈ Remove the pan from the heat and leave it to cool a little. Gradually pour on the warm water, taking great care that the sugar mixture does not splash.

≈ Return the pan to low heat to dissolve the caramel, then remove it from the heat and allow to cool.

≈ Arrange the sliced kumquats in a serving dish, and scatter the raisins over them. Pour the caramel over the fruit. Decorate with the bay leaf and serve chilled.

NUTRITION FACTS	
Amount per Serving	
Calories 284	Calories from Fat 0
	% Daily Value
Total Fat 0g	0%
Saturated Fat 0g	0%
Polyunsaturated Fat 0g	0%
Monounsaturated Fat 0g	0%
Cholesterol 0mg	0%
Sodium 14mg	0.5%
Total Carbohydrate 64g	21%
Dietary Fibre 6g	24%
Sugars 64g	0%
Protein 1g	0%

Percent daily values are based on a 2000 calorie diet

HONEY AND ORANGE FIGS

SERVES 4

This recipe offers a refreshing way to serve fresh figs.

2 tbsp clear honey
1 tbsp lemon juice
4 tbsp orange juice
4 ripe figs, sliced into rings
2 oranges, peeled and segmented
4 sprigs of mint

≈ Stir the honey into the fruit juices until it has dissolved. Put the fruit into a dish, pour the honey mixture over the fruit and stir lightly. Cover and chill for at least 1 hour.

≈ Stir gently before dividing among 4 chilled dishes. Decorate each serving with a sprig of mint.

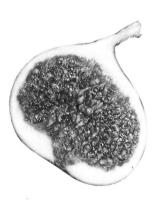

NUTRITION FACTS	
Amount per Serving	
Calories 80	Calories from Fat 0
	% Daily Value
Total Fat 0g	0%
Saturated Fat 0g	0%
Polyunsaturated Fat 0g	0%
Monounsaturated Fat 0g	0%
Cholesterol 0mg	0%
Sodium 7mg	0.3%
Total Carbohydrate 19g	6%
Dietary Fibre 3g	12%
Sugars 19g	0%
Protein 2g	0%

Percent daily values are based on a 2000 calorie diet

WATERMELON GRANITÉ

SERVES 8

1 medium-sized watermelon
50 g/2 oz icing sugar
150 ml/5 fl oz ginger ale
1 tbsp lemon or lime juice

≈ Cut into the top of the watermelon in a zig-zag pattern, then lift the top off carefully.

≈ Using a spoon, scoop out the flesh and remove all the seeds. Freeze the shell. Place the flesh in a blender in batches and blend until smooth. Pour into a bowl.

≈ Dissolve the icing sugar in the ginger ale, stir in the lemon or lime juice and add to the melon. Pour into a suitable container. Freeze until ice crystals form around the edges, then draw these into the mixture. Freeze until the whole is a mass of small crystals. Scrape into the reserved shell and serve.

TANGERINE AND GINGER SORBET

SERVES 8

8 large tangerines

1 cm/½ in piece fresh ginger, peeled
and grated

175 g/6 oz caster sugar

finely grated peel and juice of
1 lemon

finely grated peel and juice of
1 small orange

finely grated peel and juice of
½ grapefruit

1 egg white

≈ Cut the tops off the tangerines and reserve. Using a grapefruit knife, cut out the fruit. Place the empty shells in tartlet pans. Remove the seeds from the fruit and blend the pulp with the ginger. Strain into a saucepan, add the sugar and heat until dissolved. Add the grated peel and juice of the lemon, orange and grapefruit. Put into a container suitable for the freezer and freeze until just firm. Remove from the freezer and beat.

≈ Whisk the egg white until stiff and fold into the frozen mixture. Spoon into the empty shells, top each with the reserved lids, return these to the tartlet pans and freeze until firm.

NUTRITION FACTS	
Amount per Serving	
Calories 99	Calories from Fat 0
	% Daily Value
Total Fat 0g	0%
Saturated Fat 0g	0%
Polyunsaturated Fat 0g	0%
Monounsaturated Fat 0g	0%
Cholesterol 0mg	0%
Sodium 12mg	0.5%
Total Carbohydrate 25g	8%
Dietary Fibre 1g	4%
Sugars 25g	0%
Protein 1g	0%

Percent daily values are based on a 2000 calorie diet

FETTUCCINE WITH APPLE AND CINNAMON SAUCE

SERVES 6

This delightful dessert can be made with ground mixed spice as an alternative to cinnamon. For a special occasion, sprinkle each plate of pasta with a little calvados or rum before serving.

Pasta Dough

225 g/8 oz plain flour

2 tsp ground cinnamon

3 tbsp sunflower oil

1 tbsp water

2 eggs

Sauce

3–4 medium dessert apples, peeled,
    cored, and sliced

finely grated zest of 1 lemon

¼ tsp ground cinnamon

3 tbsp water, plus 150 ml/5 fl oz

3 tbsp soft light brown sugar

75 g/3 oz raisins

1 tbsp polyunsaturated margarine

2 tsp arrowroot blended with 2 tsp
    cold water

flour, to dredge

dash of sunflower oil

≈ In a large mixing bowl, combine the flour and ground cinnamon. Make a well in the centre. In a small bowl, combine the sunflower oil and water and beat well. Break the eggs into the well, and add the oil and water mixture gradually. Mix until the dough forms clumps.

≈ Turn out onto a lightly floured surface and knead the dough for about 5 minutes, adding the minimum amount of extra flour to stop the dough sticking, if necessary.

≈ Keep the pasta dough wrapped in plastic wrap to prevent it from drying out, and set aside for at least 30 minutes.

≈ To make the sauce, put the apples into a saucepan with the lemon zest, cinnamon and 3 tbsp water. Cover and cook gently until the apples have softened. Remove about half of the apple slices from the saucepan, and set aside. Place the remaining apples in a food processor or blender and purée until smooth.

≈ Return the purée to the saucepan and stir in the reserved apples, sugar, raisins, 1 tbsp margarine, arrowroot mixture and 150 ml/5 fl oz water. Cook for about 5 minutes, stirring constantly, until bubbling and thickened. Set aside.

≈ To make the fettuccine, roll out the pasta dough very thinly on a floured surface. Lightly dredge with flour, then roll up and use a sharp knife to cut the dough into thin slices. Shake out the noodles as they are cut, and pile them on a floured baking tray.

≈ To cook the fettuccine, bring a large saucepan of water to the boil and add the pasta with a dash of sunflower oil. Cook for about 3 minutes, stirring occasionally, until tender.

≈ Meanwhile, reheat the sauce. Drain the fettuccine. Stir in the sauce and serve on warmed individual plates.

NUTRITION FACTS	
Amount per Serving	
Calories 312	Calories from Fat 90
	% Daily Value
Total Fat 10g	15%
Saturated Fat 2g	10%
Polyunsaturated Fat 5g	0%
Monounsaturated Fat 3g	0%
Cholesterol 79mg	26%
Sodium 54mg	2%
Total Carbohydrate 54g	18%
Dietary Fibre 3.5g	14%
Sugars 27g	0%
Protein 6g	0%

Percent daily values are based on a 2000 calorie diet

CONTINENTAL PLUM CAKE

SERVES 6

175 g/6 oz caster sugar

175 g/6 oz polyunsaturated margarine, melted

3 eggs, separated

175 g/6 oz superfine flour, sifted

½ tsp vanilla extract

350 g/¾ lb firm, small plums, pitted and halved

icing sugar for dusting

This is a deliciously light sponge cake with a difference. For best results the eggs should be weighed and the sugar, margarine and flour should each be the same weight as the eggs. Take care not to let the margarine overheat. You can use different fruits, but choose firm types like apricots or mango.

≈ Preheat the oven to 190°C/375°F/Gas Mark 5. Line the base of a baking pan with wax paper.

≈ Beat the caster sugar and margarine together until light and fluffy. Add the vanilla extract and gradually beat in one egg yolk at a time. If it curdles, add a little flour.

≈ Whisk the egg whites until stiff and gradually fold into the creamed mixture alternately with the flour. Spoon into the prepared pan, level the surface and arrange the plums over the top.

≈ Bake for about 40–45 minutes until risen and golden and no mark is left when you press it lightly with your fingertips.

≈ Allow to cool slightly before removing from the pan and the wax paper if serving hot. Sprinkle with icing sugar and serve either hot or cold. Turn out onto a cooling rack if serving cold.

NUTRITION FACTS	
Amount per Serving	
Calories 453	Calories from Fat 252
	% Daily Value
Total Fat 28g	43%
Saturated Fat 6g	30%
Polyunsaturated Fat 11g	0%
Monounsaturated Fat 9g	0%
Cholesterol 120mg	40%
Sodium 333mg	14%
Total Carbohydrate 48g	16%
Dietary Fibre 2.5g	10%
Sugars 29g	0%
Protein 6g	0%

Percent daily values are based on a 2000 calorie diet

CITRUS JELLY

SERVES 4

A perfect way to follow a rich or substantial main dish – a three-fruit jello set around a ring of orange sections and attractively decorated with lemon-scented geranium leaves.

6 oranges

1 lemon

50 ml/2 fl oz water

1 tbsp powdered gelozone

1 lime

clear honey, to taste

Decoration

pistachio nuts

geranium leaves

≈ Using a potato peeler remove just the peel from 2 of the oranges and the lemon, leaving the pith on the fruit. Place in a saucepan with water, bring to the boil and simmer for 7–8 minutes. Break the two oranges into sections.

≈ Sprinkle the gelatine over 3 tbsp water and leave to soak for 5 minutes. Add the gelatine liquid to the pan, off the heat and stir to dissolve. Strain and discard the rind. Juice the remaining 4 oranges and lime, then place in a measuring cup and add water to make 725 ml/25 fl oz. Add to pan. Sweeten with honey.

≈ Pour the jelly into 4 individual sundae dishes, and refrigerate to set, reserving 170 ml/6 fl oz of the jelly.

≈ Arrange the orange sections on top of each jelly and pour over the remaining liquid jelly. Refrigerate to set.

≈ Decorate with pistachio nuts, and serve each dish on a plate decorated with geranium leaves.

NUTRITION FACTS	
Amount per Serving	
Calories 131	Calories from Fat 9
	% Daily Value
Total Fat 1g	1.5%
Saturated Fat 0.1g	0.5%
Polyunsaturated Fat 0.4g	0%
Monounsaturated Fat 0.5g	0%
Cholesterol 0mg	0%
Sodium 32mg	1.3%
Total Carbohydrate 26g	9%
Dietary Fibre 1g	4%
Sugars 26g	0%
Protein 5g	0%

Percent daily values are based on a 2000 calorie diet

PORTUGUESE PEACHES IN RED WINE

SERVES 6

6 peaches

1 cinnamon stick

½–¾ bottle of red wine

100 g/4 oz caster sugar

ground cinnamon, to serve

During the peach-growing season large bowls of peaches are available at the huge peach-growing estates on the Costa Azul in Portugal.

≈ Preheat the oven to 180°C/350°F/ Gas Mark 4.

≈ Pour boiling water over the peaches and leave for about 30–60 seconds; then remove with a perforated spoon and slip off the skins. If the skins are stubborn, return the peaches briefly to the water.

≈ Put the peaches into a baking dish which they just fit, tuck the cinnamon stick in between them and pour over enough wine to cover them. Sprinkle over the sugar and bake for 40–50 minutes until the peaches are tender.

≈ Remove from the oven, discard the cinnamon stick, turn the peaches over and leave to cool in the wine, turning once or twice more.

≈ Serve dusted lightly with ground cinnamon.

NUTRITION FACTS

Amount per Serving

Calories 141	Calories from Fat 1
	% Daily Value
Total Fat 0.1g	0.2%
Saturated Fat 0g	0%
Polyunsaturated Fat 0g	0%
Monounsaturated Fat 0g	0%
Cholesterol 0mg	0%
Sodium 7mg	0.3%
Total Carbohydrate 24g	8%
Dietary Fibre 1.5g	6%
Sugars 24g	0%
Protein 1g	0%

Percent daily values are based on a 2000 calorie diet

BAKED STUFFED PEACHES

SERVES 4

50 g/2 oz spongecake crumbs

50 g/2 oz ground almonds

2 tbsp caster sugar

2 tbsp dry sherry

a little polyunsaturated margarine

4 large peaches

This popular Italian dessert may be made with fresh peaches or nectarines.

≈ Preheat the oven to 180°C/350°F/ Gas Mark 4.

≈ Place the cake crumbs, almonds, sugar and sherry in a bowl and mix together. Grease a shallow ovenproof dish.

≈ Skin the peaches by dipping quickly into boiling water. Lift out with a slotted spoon and peel off the skin. Cut the peaches in half, remove the stones and fill the cavities with the almond stuffing. Place in the dish and cook for 20–30 minutes until the peaches are soft and the stuffing is lightly browned. Serve either hot or cold.

NUTRITION FACTS

Amount per Serving

Calories 209	Calories from Fat 63
	% Daily Value
Total Fat 7g	11%
Saturated Fat 1g	5%
Polyunsaturated Fat 2g	0%
Monounsaturated Fat 3g	0%
Cholesterol 56mg	19%
Sodium 36mg	1.5%
Total Carbohydrate 33g	11%
Dietary Fibre 3g	12%
Sugars 27g	0%
Protein 5g	0%

Percent daily values are based on a 2000 calorie diet

TOMATO, ORANGE AND BASIL SORBET

SERVES 6

1 l/1¾ pt tomato juice

juice of ½ lemon

2 tsp finely chopped basil

finely grated peel and juice of
    1 orange

2 drops chilli sauce

salt and pepper

2 egg whites

basil leaves, to garnish

≈ Mix together the tomato juice, lemon juice, basil, orange peel and juice and chilli sauce. Season with salt and pepper to taste. Pour into a suitable container and freeze for 1½ hours until mushy.

≈ Remove from the freezer and whisk well, then return to the freezer for a further 1 hour until it is again mushy. Whisk once more.

≈ Whisk the egg whites until stiff and fold into the tomato mixture. Return to the freezer and freeze until solid.

≈ Put in the refrigerator 30 minutes before serving. Spoon into individual dishes and garnish with basil leaves. Serve with Melba Toast.

NUTRITION FACTS	
Amount per Serving	
Calories 32	Calories from Fat 0
	% Daily Value
Total Fat 0g	0%
Saturated Fat 0g	0%
Polyunsaturated Fat 0g	0%
Monounsaturated Fat 0g	0%
Cholesterol 0mg	0%
Sodium 434mg	18%
Total Carbohydrate 6g	2%
Dietary Fibre 1.5g	6%
Sugars 6g	0%
Protein 2g	0%

Percent daily values are based on a 2000 calorie diet

GOLDEN SUMMER PUDDING

SERVES 6

This dish requires a total of 900 g/2 lb of fruit.

2 oranges

2 cups water

6 tbsp granulated sugar

2 peaches or 1 nectarine

2 mangoes

10–12 slices white bread

To decorate

slices of mango (optional)

slices of orange (optional)

≈ Remove the peel from the oranges and place in a saucepan with the water and sugar. Dissolve the sugar and cook gently for 2 minutes to extract the flavour from the orange peel. Remove the pan from the heat and discard the orange peel.

≈ Skin the peaches and mangoes and remove the stones. Cut the flesh into small dice, add to the flavoured syrup and cook to just soften the fruit, about 5 minutes. Remove from the heat.

≈ Cut 12 rounds of bread to fit the base and tops of six ramekin dishes and place a round in the base of each dish. Cut small squares of bread and use to line the sides of the dishes.

≈ Using a slotted spoon, fill each dish with the fruit, reserving the syrup to serve with the puddings. Top each with the remaining circles of bread, pressing down well. Cover each tightly with plastic wrap and leave to chill overnight.

≈ To serve, remove carefully from the dishes, spoon the remaining syrup over and decorate, if desired, with extra slices of mango or orange.

NUTRITION FACTS	
Amount per Serving	
Calories 280	Calories from Fat 9
	% Daily Value
Total Fat 1g	1.5%
Saturated Fat 0.3g	1.5%
Polyunsaturated Fat 0.3g	0%
Monounsaturated Fat 0.2g	0%
Cholesterol 0mg	0%
Sodium 317mg	13%
Total Carbohydrate 65g	22%
Dietary Fibre 1.5g	6%
Sugars 37g	0%
Protein 6g	0%

Percent daily values are based on a 2000 calorie diet

FRESH FRUIT DESSERT CAKE

SERVES 8

2 eggs

50 ml/2 fl oz milk

2 tbsp honey

2 tbsp treacle

175 g/6 oz wholemeal flour

1 tsp baking powder

1 tsp bicarbonate of soda

1 tsp cinnamon

pinch of salt

450 g/1 lb peaches

225 g/½ lb plums

225 g/½ lb cherries

100 g/4 oz walnuts, chopped

a little margarine

fresh fruit to decorate

To serve

whipped cream*

≈ Preheat the oven to 200°C/400°F/ Gas Mark 6.

≈ Beat the eggs with the milk. Stir in the honey and treacle. Stir in the rest of the dry ingredients and mix well.

≈ Remove the stones and chop the fruit. Mix it into the batter with the nuts. Pour into a greased and floured 20 cm/ 8 inch cake pan with a removable bottom (spring form cake pan) and bake for 50–60 minutes until set in the middle. Dot with margarine towards the end of the cooking time to prevent the top drying out.

≈ Allow to cool in the pan. Chill and decorate with fresh fruit.

NUTRITION FACTS	
Amount per Serving	
Calories 240	Calories from Fat 100
	% Daily Value
Total Fat 11g	17%
Saturated Fat 1g	5%
Polyunsaturated Fat 6g	0%
Monounsaturated Fat 2g	0%
Cholesterol 60mg	20%
Sodium 31mg	1%
Total Carbohydrate 30g	10%
Dietary Fibre 5.5g	22%
Sugars 16g	0%
Protein 8g	0%

Percent daily values are based on a 2000 calorie diet

GRAPE CUSTARDS

SERVES 4

225 g/½ lb seedless red grapes

4 egg yolks

3 tbsp caster sugar

4 tbsp marsala, madeira, or sweet
sherry

NUTRITION FACTS	
Amount per Serving	
Calories 174	Calories from Fat 54

	% Daily Value
Total Fat 6g	9%
Saturated Fat 2g	10%
Polyunsaturated Fat 1g	0%
Monounsaturated Fat 2g	0%
Cholesterol 202mg	67%
Sodium 13mg	0.5%
Total Carbohydrate 25g	8%
Dietary Fibre 0.5g	2%
Sugars 25g	0%
Protein 3g	0%

Percent daily values are based on a 2000 calorie diet

≈ Wash the grapes and divide among 4 individual glasses.

≈ Place the egg yolks in a bowl. Beat lightly, add the sugar and wine and mix together. Place the bowl over a pan of hot water and whisk, for about 10 minutes, until the mixture is thick and creamy.

≈ Divide the mixture among the glasses and serve at once while still warm with sponge fingers.

120

LYCHEE AND LIME SORBET

SERVES 4

450 g/1 lb fresh lychees

juice of 1 lime

25 g/1 oz icing sugar, sifted

1 egg white

≈ Peel the lychees and remove the stones. Place the flesh in a blender with the lime juice and icing sugar. Process until smooth.

≈ Pour into a container suitable for the freezer, freeze until slushy, then beat well. Repeat this twice.

≈ Whisk the egg white until firm and fold into the sorbet. Freeze for several hours until solid.

≈ Serve in small scoops with slices of fresh mango or other suitable fruit, or with another fruit sorbet such as mango or kiwi.

NUTRITION FACTS	
Amount per Serving	
Calories 201	Calories from Fat 0
	% Daily Value
Total Fat 0g	0%
Saturated Fat 0g	0%
Polyunsaturated Fat 0g	0%
Monounsaturated Fat 0g	0%
Cholesterol 0mg	0%
Sodium 18mg	0.75%
Total Carbohydrate 52g	17%
Dietary Fibre 1g	4%
Sugars 52g	0%
Protein 2g	0%

Percent daily values are based on a 2000 calorie diet

1 small melon

3 kiwi

175 g/6 oz green grapes

1 green apple

2 guavas

6 leaves of gelozone

450 ml/16 fl oz water

150 ml/5 fl oz fruit cordial

Sugar Syrup

175 g/6 oz granulated sugar

450 ml/16 fl oz water

NUTRITION FACTS	
Amount per Serving	
Calories 246	Calories from Fat 5
	% Daily Value
Total Fat 0.5g	0.8%
Saturated Fat 0g	0%
Polyunsaturated Fat 0g	0%
Monounsaturated Fat 0g	0%
Cholesterol 0mg	0%
Sodium 49mg	2%
Total Carbohydrate 60g	20%
Dietary Fibre 3.5g	14%
Sugars 60g	0%
Protein 4g	0%

Percent daily values are based on a 2000 calorie diet

MELON, KIWI FRUIT AND GRAPE SALAD

SERVES 6

This is a refreshing salad made with exotic fruits of the same colour mixed with fragrant jelly.

≈ Soak the gelatine in half the water for 15 minutes. Add the remaining water, place in a saucepan and heat gently to dissolve. Allow to cool slightly before adding the cordial. Rinse a 18 cm/7-inch shallow square pan with water and pour in the jelly mixture. Leave in a cold place to set.

≈ To make the syrup, put the sugar and water in a saucepan and heat until the sugar has dissolved. Boil rapidly for 2–3 minutes until slightly syrupy. Remove from the heat and cool.

≈ Cut the melon into balls or cubes and place in a large serving bowl. Peel and slice the kiwi. Wash the grapes, halve and seed if necessary. Wash and core the apple and cut into slices. Add all these fruits to the bowl with the cooled syrup. Peel the guavas, halve and scoop out the seeds. Slice and add to the salad.

≈ Quickly dip the pan of jelly into hot water and turn out onto damp wax paper. Cut into large cubes. Add to the salad just before serving.

---

225 g/8 oz caster sugar

4 tbsp water

225 g/8 oz blanched almonds, ground

few drops of orange flower or rose water or almond extract

icing sugar

NUTRITION FACTS	
Amount per Serving (each)	
Calories 81	Calories from Fat 45
	% Daily Value
Total Fat 5g	8%
Saturated Fat 0.5g	2.5%
Polyunsaturated Fat 1g	0%
Monounsaturated Fat 3g	0%
Cholesterol 0mg	0%
Sodium 2mg	0%
Total Carbohydrate 8.5g	3%
Dietary Fibre 1g	4%
Sugars 8g	0%
Protein 2g	0%

Percent daily values are based on a 2000 calorie diet

MARZIPAN CANDIES

MAKES 24

Marzipan is the starting-point for many Portuguese candies, which are a legacy of the Moorish occupation. The paste may be coloured, using food colourings and moulded into shapes to resemble fruits, animals and so on, then put into small paper cases. The freshness of the almonds is important.

≈ Heat the sugar and water gently in a small saucepan until the sugar has dissolved; then boil to make a light syrup.

≈ Add the almonds and stir over a low heat until very thick and dry. Mix in the orange flower or rose water or almond extract, turn on to a lightly oiled surface and leave to cool.

≈ Sift a thin coating of icing sugar over the work surface and form the almond paste into the desired shapes. Leave to dry for a few days in a dry, airy place.

HONEY, ORANGE AND ALMOND TAGLIATELLE

SERVES 4

Pasta tossed in a honey syrup makes a perfect pasta dish to end a meal.

225 g/½ lb dried egg tagliatelle

dash of sunflower oil

4 oranges

5 tbsp clear honey

3 tbsp soft light brown sugar

1 tbsp lemon juice

2 tbsp polyunsaturated margarine

75 g/3 oz flaked almonds

≈ Bring a large saucepan of water to the boil and add the tagliatelle with a dash of sunflower oil. Cook for about 8–10 minutes, stirring occasionally, until tender. Drain, and set aside.

≈ While the pasta is cooking, peel and slice three of the oranges, and cut the slices in half. Squeeze the juice from the remaining orange into a small saucepan. Add the honey, sugar and lemon juice.

Bring to the boil, stirring to dissolve the sugar, and simmer for 1–2 minutes until syrupy.

≈ Melt the margarine in a pan, and fry the flaked almonds until golden. Stir in the tagliatelle and honey syrup, heat through, then quickly stir in the orange slices. Serve immediately.

≈ Pare strips of zest from the skin of one orange, and cut into thin "julienne" strips to garnish.

NUTRITION FACTS	
Amount per Serving	
Calories 563	Calories from Fat 190
	% Daily Value
Total Fat 21g	32%
Saturated Fat 3.5g	17.5%
Polyunsaturated Fat 6g	0%
Monounsaturated Fat 10g	0%
Cholesterol 17mg	6%
Sodium 170mg	7%
Total Carbohydrate 86g	29%
Dietary Fibre 8g	32%
Sugars 47g	0%
Protein 12g	0%

Percent daily values are based on a 2000 calorie diet

ALMOND PETITS FOURS

MAKES ABOUT 24

This is an excellent dessert base, onto which you can pop any number of enticing little delicacies.

4 egg whites

100 g/¼ lb ground almonds

100 g/¼ lb caster sugar

4 tbsp plain flour

≈ Beat the egg whites very stiffly.

≈ Mix the almonds, sugar and flour together and gently fold in the egg whites.

≈ Pipe the mixture onto a baking sheet; you should have 24 bases. Bake at 200°C/400°F/Gas Mark 6 for about 8 minutes.

≈ Top the individual bases with puréed apple and cinnamon with a baked almond on top, or melted chocolate; or a fresh berry; and so on.

NUTRITION FACTS	
Amount per Serving (each)	
Calories 55	Calories from Fat 18
	% Daily Value
Total Fat 2g	3%
Saturated Fat 0.2g	1%
Polyunsaturated Fat 0.5g	0%
Monounsaturated Fat 1g	0%
Cholesterol 0mg	0%
Sodium 11mg	0.5%
Total Carbohydrate 7g	2%
Dietary Fibre 0.5g	2%
Sugars 5g	0%
Protein 2g	0%

Percent daily values are based on a 2000 calorie diet

INDEX